60 Ways
to reach a
Difficult and Defiant Child

---

a guide for
COUNSELORS

1-25-10

Dr. James Sutton

60 Ways
to reach a
Difficult and Defiant Child

by Dr. James Sutton

published and distributed by:

Friendly Oaks Publications
PO Box 662
Pleasanton, TX 78064
830.569.3586
fax: 830.281.2617

Preliminary Statement:
   The insights, suggestions, strategies and interventions included in this book are as accurate, purposeful, sensitive and responsible as the author and publisher can make them. This book is intended to be a resource for counselors and therapists who wish to build upon their own training and experiences.

   The author and publisher shall have neither liability nor responsibility to any person or entity with respect to any loss or damage caused, or alleged to be caused, directly or indirectly, by the information contained in this book. Any reader who wishes not to be bound by this Preliminary Statement may return this book to the publisher for a full and complete refund.

International Standard Book Number: 978-1-878878-75-5

TABLE OF CONTENTS:

INTRODUCTION:

I have enjoyed the opportunity afforded me over the years to work with young people. What better investment into the best possible future could there be than making a difference in young lives? What greater accomplishment could there be than seeing a life you've influenced go out and count in a real and rigorous world? That's the mountain top for counselors, and it feels great to spend a little time there, doesn't it?

But mountains run into valleys. If you were to ask me, "Do you enjoy working with young people *all* the time?" I'd have to be honest. I don't. I can painfully recall moments that seemed to stretch into days, moments punctuated by circumstances that would hardly be described as "enjoyable." It was likely those times were spent with difficult or defiant youngsters. They tried my patience and tested my skills. They were the force behind this guide.

I started out by putting together a short supplement (three pages) to my full-day training programs for educators on working with difficult and defiant youngsters. This supplement focused on tips for providing support services to youngsters "resistant" to the more typical, cordial and interactive approaches to counseling or therapy. It became a project of sorts, something that, with a lot of outside help and feedback, took on a will and a direction of its own. So, pages and pages later, here it is.

If you've had the experience of working with a child you're expected to perform miracles with (only you're coming up a little short in the miracle department), there are some ideas in here that can help. They're included here because they have worked in "real life" situations in the trenches of daily work with children and adolescents. After all, isn't that the best way to know if an idea is any good or not?

Some of these ideas and interventions deal with a child's normal apprehension about seeing a counselor or therapist, especially for the first time. Some strategies deepen rapport and establish a working trust, while others are intended to deflect some of the youngster's defensive behaviors. A few of the interventions are diagnostic in that they informally assess a youngster's affect, how he structures thought and how he manifests anxiety. There are even interventions on acceptance and forgiveness, as well as interventions designed to show youngsters how to interpret and evaluate their own progress and move from there. (I've always felt a counselor's job was 50% inspiration and 50% inoculation.)

Since the discussion in this book is about difficult and defiant youngsters, we'll also consider ways to pick up on insincerity, avoidance, manipulation and outright dishonesty. (For several years, I worked part-time with adolescents placed in juvenile detention or who were on juvenile probation. These kids were "ordered" to counseling. Now there's a challenge!) No child is ever a lost cause, but our time is too valuable to waste, especially if there *is* a way to reach that youngster. Often there is.

What you'll find here are interventions that have been used not only within the school setting (I began as a Special Education teacher, then later a school psychologist, advanced addiction specialist, a counselor and a licensed psychologist), but in *every* environment where a therapist or counselor would work with a child: foster care, group home and therapeutic group home placement, residential treatment, hospitalization and drug and alcohol rehabilitation. There is opportunity here for broad application.

As I was wrapping up this guide, it occurred to me that much of the material here would be excellent for teachers and direct support staff as they might work with a youngster on an Individualized Education Plan (or a Behavior Plan) for emotional and behavioral improvement. Keep that in mind as you move through this material. I wish you life-changing success.

—JDS

1

"Can I Stay Here with You—FOREVER?"

(FOREVER? How about 'til Tuesday?)

Okay, so you won't ever hear a difficult or defiant youngster saying something like this, unless he's looking to hide out 'til the coast clears (a *distinct* possibility we'll look at later). If you *do* hear it coming from one of these kids, send him to the nurse—he's probably running a fever.

Seriously, the difficult and defiant child represents a benchmark of sorts to a counselor or therapist. Against this youngster we measure our successes, those kids that are *easy* to like and even *easier* to work with. I'm talking about the sort of child who, when you help her, makes it her duty to be your friend for life. Frankly, she is the sort of youngster that keeps you in the business. And, if your experiences are like mine, you don't have to be the world's greatest counselor to make a difference in her life. Things just fall into place easily. Just about *any* course or direction you take with her works. If all your counseling cases were like her, you'd have the world's greatest job! If.

In contrast, there's the kid who can send you into early retirement. Working with this child can be as much fun as having your gums scraped. This youngster can make a session so silent and painful (for *both* of you) that you begin to seriously wonder if *Dairy Queen* is hiring. Speaking for myself, there have been those times when this youngster, the difficult and defiant one, has caused me to second-guess my skills and abilities. That hurt, but it also motivated me to get better. (If you haven't "been there," just wait; you *will* be.)

It's a given these youngsters can be tough. Don't kick yourself too hard when things don't work out like you want. Instead, prepare to get better. Prepare to make a difference.

2

"Stop CONFUSING Me—It Messes Me Up"

(Yes, but you like it, don't you?)

Okay, it's the very first session with a youngster who is majoring in trouble. Maybe he's at your door right now. What's running through his mind? What is he expecting?

I can tell you. Pretty much without exception, he's expecting PAIN. He's dead certain this will be an uncomfortable experience in some way. (Is it possible that, just maybe, the referring teacher would like for you to *give* him some pain?) Chances are he's not standing there because he is overwhelmed with the magnitude of his inability to control his behavior and defiance. He's standing there because he has a boot in his behind. (Well, not literally, but you get the idea.)

Coming to your office is painful in itself for him. Now he's bracing for the next round of discomfort. What happens next, however, is something *you* can control, not the teacher, principal or parent. Will it make a difference? Bet on it.

Joel Weldon, a very powerful platform speaker shared some advice with me once that works miracles in many different situations. He said, "Find out what everyone else is doing—then *don't* do it!"

So, if the youngster's expecting an uncomfortable experience of some sort, challenge the expectation. Make it painless, maybe even a little fun.

He'll be thoroughly confused for the whole session.

3

"You Want MY Help?"

(Of course, I do.)

I believe it was Dr. Joyce Brothers who once said, "The quickest way to develop a relationship with someone is to ask them for a small favor." She would often emphasize the word "small" as being important. Small favors are not ingratiating, nor do they require repayment. (A person in our checkout line at the grocery store will give us three cents when we're short on change, with no expectation of being repaid. A loan of $30.00, however, would be a different story.)

Here's how it works. Let's say you greet the youngster at the door and share a quick introduction. (So far, so good; no pain yet.) Then you say you need to make a couple of notes, and ask her if she would put a small stack of books into a box for you while you wrap up.

It's a simple task, and my guess is she'll jump right into it because putting books in a box is a diversion, a pleasant shift from what she was expecting. But it's also a distraction, a distraction from pain.

If you walk the child to your office, consider raking a dozen books or so off your bookshelf onto the floor as you leave to get her. Upon walking into your office you could say, "Oh my goodness, these books fell off that shelf. Would you help me put them back?" I've also asked students to help me clear a corner of my desk so we could work, or even move the furniture around in the office so we could be more "comfortable."

In addition to such a move or gesture being a distraction from the negative, the child is exercising compliance for you (that's worth noting), and it provides an opportunity for you to express your appreciation to her.

That's something this child might not have heard from an adult for some time. It's not a bad start, if you can make it work.

I used a spin on this idea working with children and adolescents at a group home. I would ask them if they would help me bring in a couple of boxes from my car. I figured a youngster would do most anything other than be anxious and uncomfortable in my office for the first time.

On days when I intended to use this strategy, I parked my vehicle half a block away. I would make it a point to have two identical boxes in the trunk, one for me and one for the child. I had a chance to visit with the youngster as we slowly strolled back to my office with the boxes. This helped to settle the child and, of course, I praised his willingness to help me.

My next client would help me carry a couple of boxes *to* my car. (On those days, the boxes got quite a workout.)

4

"How Do You DO That?"

(Practice, practice, practice)

A counselor friend of mine showed me a great little trick that creates a positive diversion from what the youngster is expecting in coming to the counselor for the first time. Actually, he mesmerizes them; he's a juggler. He can juggle anything. As a child walks into his office, he picks up apples, oranges, staplers—whatever, and works his magic.

It works. It also becomes the focal point for early discussion—something safe and observable. He sometimes offers to teach the youngster to juggle (starting off with scarves), which is also a great rapport-builder. Obviously, he doesn't use this with all students, nor does he wear out the juggling as an intervention by using it too often.

It might not be juggling for you, but what kind of talent can you showcase with ease? (I used to keep a classical guitar in my office on a small stand. If things became too quiet, I'd pick it up and play. Sometimes they'd start talking to get me to *stop*!)

5

"It's OVER ... Already?"

(Time just flies when you're having fun.)

If I can have a youngster leaving my office thinking, "That wasn't half bad," I have accomplished most of my goals for a first session. In fact, here's my primary goal for a first session: **I want to get them back for the SECOND session.** And I want them to feel better about coming to the second session.

One excellent way to accomplish this is to make the first session so short the youngster doesn't have *time* to become too uncomfortable.

Jimmy came into my office one day for a first visit. Like just about all difficult youngsters, he was not a "volunteer." He had been sent. He hardly

13

expected a favorable reception as he pushed through the double glass doors leading into the waiting room outside my office.

You know the look—a deer in the headlights.

I quickly introduced myself and asked him to sit down on the couch in the waiting area (not in my office; we were alone). I had him sit where he could clearly see the clock over my right shoulder.

I apologized to Jimmy, sharing that I could only see him for about ten minutes because I had a plane to catch. I told him I just wanted to introduce myself and visit with him a bit, then I'd have to let him go until next time. I asked him if that would be okay, for us to have a very short session as our first visit.

He would have been fine with *no* session, right? In a flash all of his preconceptions of a difficult, hand-wringing experience began to wither. His thoughts: "Hey, however bad this gets, I only have to stand TEN MINUTES of it." And I set it up so he could count down the time himself, if he wanted to.

6

"Why Am I Here?"

(That's a fair question.)

As we all are all aware, the difficult and defiant youngster is not exactly a prime candidate for self-referral. If he really doesn't know why he's in your office, the direct approach is probably the best.

If a teacher or administrator has made a referral, chances are it has to do with behavioral concerns or noncompliance (the *absence* of the desired behavior). The child might know why he's seeing you, he might not know, or he might know and doesn't want to say.

I've always felt that a vague explanation on my part ("Oh, I just wanted to visit with you and get to know you a little better; I see a lot of students at this school") was a bit dishonest and misleading. A bright youngster, especially one who already has a good idea what the situation is (whether he says so or not), might even think you're lying.

I would prefer to put the cards on the table, then remove them until things settle a bit:

> *Ted, your teacher spoke with me. She is concerned about the way you talk to classmates and how you seem angry and upset most of the time in class. She asked me if I would visit with you, and your mom said it was okay. Actually, your mom has some of the same concerns. Ted, I suppose you don't have to agree with what I just said, but it is important to me that you understand what I just explained. Do you understand* (nodding my head)? *Good. Hey, would you like to help me with something?*

The "help me with something" would be some sort of minor diversion. (One time I had a cage of two white rabbits I was delivering to someone before going home. It was a great built-in diversion and rapport-builder.) It could have been the boxes in my car.

Before the youngster leaves the first session, or early in the second, I like to reverify why I'm seeing him—using *his* perspective:

Ted, when I explained earlier why I was seeing you in my office, you said you understood what I said. It's pretty important to me that you do. Can you tell me what I told you?

I then reinforce or restate. It presents a great opening for getting into the issues when I ask, "Is that the way it is?" or "Does that sound right to you?"

7

"It's Okay if I'm a LITTLE Nervous?"

(Only if it's not contagious)

If a youngster is a bit anxious, and it's an obvious thing, it's fine to put that on the table also:

You know, Mary, it's really common for students to be a little nervous or anxious when they come to the counselor for the first time. It's normal, really. Were you just a little anxious coming here today, not exactly knowing what to expect?

A really honest child will say, "Yeah, a little, I guess." It's your opening to say with a smile, "Yeah, I thought so. You look pretty normal to me."

But I've worked with kids who felt they were supposed to be bulletproof (mostly the difficult and defiant ones). They denied being anxious at all, probably feeling it was some sort of curse (something we'll look at more later).

It's possible to use the denial to your advantage, but it carries a subtle load of sarcasm. Still, it might be worth a shot:

You're not even a LITTLE anxious? I guess that means you're NOT normal! I have a hard time believing you're not normal. You've got to explain that one to me. Can you help me understand why you're not normal?

This questioning puts them into a bind of sorts. Most youngsters wouldn't dream of "I'm not normal" ever coming out of their mouths, yet to agree they *are* normal means to admit to some discomfort (a "weakness"). Watch how they handle that one. It can be interesting.

I would recommend that you not push too hard, however. It can damage rapport. On the other hand, if I'm working with especially difficult and defiant students, I *do* want to push their buttons a bit. Just be aware that, whenever you offer an "are you normal" or "are you a little nervous" option, there will be youngsters who will jump on a third possibility: "Why are you being so MEAN to me?" Been there; done that.

8

"I Don't HAVE a Problem!"

(But my work is ABOUT problems.)

You've heard this one a zillion times, maybe *two* zillion. The youngster is in your office because of a rotten attitude, disrespect and lousy behavior, but *she* doesn't have a problem. The sad part is the youngster *believes* what she is saying. I used to get this a lot when I saw youngsters who were referred through juvenile probation.

(Talk about checking out job openings at *Dairy Queen*; these kids can be tough.)

But let's face it, counseling is *problem-generated*. It's the nature of the work. I've never had a young person come up to me and say, "I am deliriously happy and successful. Can you help me understand why?" *Not going to happen.*

If counseling is problem-generated, what do I do with a child or adolescent who doesn't have any? Simple; we *find* one. Just because a youngster says he doesn't have a problem doesn't mean there aren't a few problems hanging around somewhere. They're just not hanging around *inside* of him. (If you're thinking, "What's the difference?" just know it makes a *big* difference to the youngster.)

When you ask the question, "What's your biggest problem at school; what caused you the most difficulty and trouble?" the difficult and defiant student will always personalize it. "It's the assistant principal; she hates me," he might say.

At this point you could switch to an emphasis on empowerment, on what the youngster could do to "change" the behavior of Mrs. Smith, the assistant principal. Of course this kid will think you have lost your mind to even suggest such a thing. "How could I change her?" he might ask. There's your opening:

> *It's easy, really. The next time you see Mrs. Smith in the hallway, walk up to her and say, "Good morning, Mrs. Smith. I hope you have a nice day." That will change her behavior toward you at that moment. And if you keep doing it, her behavior toward you will keep changing. Now the first time or two you say it, you might not really mean it that much. But if'll you look and sound like you mean it, that's how you can change Mrs. Smith's behavior. In fact, I'll guarantee it, if you'll really work at it.*

18

Of course, you don't tell the student that you're also working with Mrs. Smith. She knows you are working on entry-level social skills with this youngster and, when he does or says something even close to appropriate, she is to heavily reinforce it.

If you try this little intervention, you'll find the youngster not only gets better at it, he slowly becomes more sincere. When people are treated well and regarded with respect, magic happens. But you've got to jump-start the process.

It's not a perfect intervention, but it is problem-focused and a move in the right direction.

9

"It DOESN'T Bother Me!"

(Are you sure about that?)

Denial is a protective mechanism; it guards our sanity. Be very careful in how you confront a youngster who is in denial. If you push reality too hard, you could create additional problems.

I recall a story about a 16-year-old girl who lost her grandmother. They had been very close. It just so happens that her grandmother had been a buyer for a large department store chain.

As soon as the word got out, her friends tried to comfort her, expressing their concern and condolences over her loss.

"I don't know where you heard that rumor," she said to them. "She's *not* dead. She's in Europe on a buying trip."

Granny was DEAD! The girl's response was an attempt to psychologically come to grips with the loss by buying some time to absorb it. She eventually came around to both address and accept the loss of her grandmother. She was fine.

If a youngster's behaviors, interactions and academic performance seem appropriate to the circumstances, I wouldn't worry too much about some initial denial. On the other hand, if a youngster is denying *and* falling apart, it probably means she doesn't even believe her denial. It's time to worry.

10

"It Doesn't Bother Me THAT Much"

(Minimization is "leaky" denial.)

In many ways, minimization is more difficult to deal with than denial because a youngster can minimize for 50 years.

There could be a couple of reasons why a student would minimize the impact of an emotional event. It could be a way to avoid looking at or discussing painful stuff. If a counselor puts off discussing the issue because the youngster minimizes it, the issue could eat the child alive.

There is another possibility. Youngsters who feel they *must* remain tough and bulletproof (difficult and defiant youngsters often fall into this category) feel they can't afford any emotional baggage that pulls them down. Denial and minimization are their handiest defense against what they perceive as yet more pain and vulnerability. They feel that even quality suffering and getting through the issues are luxuries they can't afford.

It has always amazed me at just how surprised these youngsters are when they get an authentic glimpse of the power of what bothers them.

20

An example. I was doing group therapy at a residential treatment center one day. In the circle with me were about a dozen emotionally disturbed adolescent females. One girl was asked if it bothered her that her mother dumped her shortly after adopting her. (The girl tried to burn the house down, not exactly a way to show her gratitude to a new mom.) "Not really," she replied. "It doesn't bother me much at all."

"Sandy," I said (not her real name), "does it bother you this much." (I patted the empty seat next to me.) "Or does it bother you THIS MUCH!" (I screamed it out and hit the chair with both hands, full force.) After we all recovered our wits, and after I assured the secretarial staff in the other room that they *didn't* have to call in the National Guard, we discussed minimization.

That remains one of my best therapy sessions *ever*.

II

"I Really DON'T Remember!"

(I believe you.)

We've all experienced the situation in which we ask a youngster a question about her experiences (especially something that happened some time ago), only to hear, "I don't know," or "I don't remember."

There's a tendency with some adults to say, "Oh, yes you *do* remember, and you're going to tell me *now*."

This response puts the child in the driver's seat because there's *no way* to prove what she knows or doesn't know. Besides, we know all individuals tend to repress traumatic memories, so "I don't remember" could be a

100% valid and truthful response. To continue to press for "the truth" from this youngster either encourages her to lie or suggests we believe she is not being truthful with us. Either way, the relationship will suffer.

One experienced counselor suggested this response:

Yes, but if you DID know, what would you say?

She was kidding, of course—I think.

Here's where patience can pay off. There's no need to press. Memory usually gets better as rapport improves and as a youngster becomes more comfortable.

12

"I Don't WANT your Help!"

(No one wants to NEED help.)

For the difficult and defiant youngster especially, the whole notion of "help" is a bad thing. It implies a need, and need implies vulnerability. Although there might be glaring need, a lot of youngsters (not just the difficult and defiant ones) don't want to face that reality. For that matter, neither do a lot adults. (How about the guy who won't stop and ask for directions? Heaven forbid it might mean he doesn't have a *clue* as to where he is!)

I cannot tell you how many times I have attempted to work with students who preferred to continue failing in a "regular" classroom than receive Special Education assistance in another place. Changing to another class meant another kind of failure to the student.

Not to beat the point to death, but I had another experience that really shed light on this notion of need and help. A residential treatment facility in San Antonio, Texas, where I served as a consultant, received a proclamation from the mayor on its service to young people. Down in the proclamation were a few words that described our young clients and their families, words like "dysfunctional." The proclamation caught the attention of one of the adolescents there. The more she read, the more upset she became.

This whole concept of need and help is important enough that clarifying and accepting it should be a specific goal in counseling. You might try a question like, "You know, it's pretty normal to need help with something once in a while. Can you think of a time in your life when you needed some help, and you were glad to receive it?" The advantage to this question is that the youngster can even reference a time when she was very young, if she wishes, like help in tying her shoes or learning to ride a bike. That's fine, because the idea is to encourage the youngster to recognize her *need* for the help at that time.

Eventually it would be the goal to get around to the real issue. It's not needing help that is so uncomfortable, it's the realization that there are some things I *can't* do for myself. I am "weakened" by that vulnerability, and it hurts to look at it. That's the *real* issue. (I love to tell youngsters that I really *don't* have to wear glasses. I only have to wear them if I want to *see*! That usually brings a chuckle or two.)

Medical help could be a good place to start, since youngsters will usually recognize it as the most valid sort of help. I haven't met a youngster yet who was up to removing his own appendix.

Recognition of a need for help and acceptance of help from others is *much* easier to discuss in a group setting because there's generally someone in the group who can and will validate both. (Isn't it interesting how some youngsters will accept a notion if it comes from a peer, but not if it comes from *you*?)

I believe it is important to assess a youngster's recognition of need as it would apply to adding them to your counseling roll in the first place. Your time is limited and valuable. Why would you want to spend much of it on a youngster who simply isn't ready to see it as a resource? This doesn't mean that I *wouldn't* work with the child. It means that, if I could only add one or two students to my caseload at this time, it might *not* be the child who sees no need for my assistance. (By the way, strong denial of a need for counseling assistance could be one indicator of an emerging personality disorder.) This is why it is so critical that a counselor assess a child's receptiveness to counseling *before* that counselor is signed up as a related service on an IEP.

13

"Are You Talking to ME?"

(Uh—yes, I believe I am.)

Ever attempt to work with a student who looked at you with a puzzled expression and wondered why on earth he was even in your office in the first place? I suppose this is a combination of dealing with denial and a refusal of assistance lightly salted with a little gamesmanship. The kid *could* be putting you on, playing dumb in order to find out what *you* know. (I saw this a lot while working with youngsters in juvenile detention.)

With this youngster, I'd fall back on indisputable facts (discipline referrals, excessive absences or tardies, fights on the playground, visits of the juvenile probation officer, or even *good* reports) and go from there. In fact, I'd make copies of the discipline referrals and put them out on the table as I talk to the student. (You don't have to worry about coming up with a problem to work on when you're both staring at *six* of them.)

14

"You AGREE with Me?"

(I'm looking for some common ground.)

From the onset, the difficult and defiant student figures to struggle with you because that's how she wins with adults. She is both uncomfortable and intrigued when you *don't* struggle. This is especially important early on in the first counseling session.

Since this particular youngster is just itching to disagree with you, ask her questions that *force* "yes" responses. If you can string together three or four of those in the first 90 seconds with this student, you've developed a positive pattern of interaction that is likely a unique experience for her. (It might not last, but it's not a bad place to start.)

Ask demographic questions that have only one answer: "Yes." Some examples:

Aren't you going to have a birthday in a couple of weeks?

You have a little sister in Mrs. Adams' class, don't you?

Your grandmother is the greeter at Wal-Mart, right?

Didn't your family just move over to Maple Street?

If I can get four "Yes" responses in a roll, it helps the fifth one. There's nothing magic about this strategy, but what do you have to lose?

Obviously, one has to be careful agreeing with a difficult and defiant student. It can lead to what psychologists call "splitting," whereby a youngster uses you a leverage against other adults. It's flattering to hear a child say, "You're the only adult in this whole school who understands me," but be *very* careful. The easiest way for this child to win is to pit the adults against each other.

It can be helpful to agree with the youngster, so long as it doesn't provide them ammunition for her own purposes. I have found that I can agree with a youngster's sense of frustration without agreeing with her behavior. ("I'll be you were pretty upset when Mr. Johnson told you that you wouldn't be going outside at lunch break for two weeks.")

15

"Hey, I Can USE This!"

(You're back, AGAIN?)

Whenever a youngster needs to see you on an emergency basis, you shouldn't have to worry about coming up with a problem. It's right there. But what if the youngster seeing you on an emergency basis *is* the problem?

Although excessively needy youngsters will often want to see the counselor continually (or *live* in the counselor's office), what about the child who uses the counselor as a way to avoid something else—like academics?

Derrik was one of those students. I received a call from the elementary school that Derrik wanted to see me—an emergency. I met with him in the school bookroom (why we met there is a *long* story).

"Derrik, what's wrong?" I asked, concern etched all over my face.

"I miss my dad," he explained tearfully, dripping on the books. He had me a little misty at that point. He went on to tell me that his folks were divorced.

"And how long has your dad been gone?"

"SEVEN YEARS!"

I had just been had. I found out later that the substitute teacher was asking the students to read aloud. Derrik had trouble with reading, so he started a brush fire of sorts. It worked for this crafty fourth grader.

In these situations it bears investigating what the student might be trying to avoid by coming to your office. If there is a genuine emergency, it should be obvious and not contrived. If it seems contrived, consider saying something like, "That sounds like something that could wait until our regular visit on Thursday. What's the emergency?"

16

"Part of Your Job, Right?

(You've got me on that one.)

Occasionally you'll met a youngster who is arrogant bordering on grandiose. His plan is to put as much distance between him and you as possible, and he's good at it. A dialog might go something like this:

Don't they pay you to work with me?

Yes, they pay me to be a counselor here.

Well, I'm not being paid to work with you, so why should I?

If this kind of arrogance causes you to feel a little warm around the collar, that's *exactly* the youngster's intent. But it can be his way of letting you know he has trouble with closeness, the sort of closeness that counseling can require. The *real* issue could be trust.

My gut-level response would be to use humor to deflect the problem:

Yeah, I tried doing it for free once, but they kept repossessing my car!

If you want to see if the youngster can *take* a joke (more on that later), you might respond with something like this:

Yes, but they don't pay me nearly enough—especially RIGHT NOW!

17

"That's NOT True!"

(Then prove me wrong.)

Whenever we offer an interpretation of a youngster's problem or behavior, we can open ourselves to attack. But sometimes it's a necessary risk.

Once, while working with a 17-year-old girl, I suggested to her that her life was getting more and more out of her control.

"That's NOT true," she replied on the verge of tears.

"Well, your boyfriend broke up with you, your boss is going to fire you if you show up late again to your after-school job, and your folks told me you're failing two subjects in school right now. If you had the ability to fix those problems, wouldn't you have done it already?" (Please don't misinterpret me here. I don't *like* this kind of confrontation, but it's sometimes necessary.)

Unable to deny the facts, she took a common option and went after me:

"Why are you being so MEAN to me? she sobbed.

It actually turned out to be a very good session. She decided the easiest of the three problems to fix was to show to work on time or quit the job. The boyfriend problem turned out to be a blessing in disguise as he was shortly thereafter busted for dealing drugs. She finally realized that, with a step-by-step plan, she could deal with most all of the issues in her life.

18

"A Little at a Time, Please"

(Okay, I'll get a smaller spoon.)

Sometimes its better to deal with issues in smaller bites. (Which is why I've never been a fan of the 50-minute hour. It's much too long for some youngsters—and for *me*! The notion of shorter sessions, however, drives managed care crazy because it messes up their billing models.)

Can you imagine saying to a youngster, "We're going to spend an hour now talking about things that are extremely painful for you. Ready—go!" And yet I believe that is close to how some youngsters perceive it.

We don't have to beat kids up with mental health, regardless of what the medical insurance folks say. Besides, those models don't really apply in the school environment anyway.

It's fine to help a youngster through some troublesome issues, but there are times when it is best to redirect to something else, then come back to it later. As a counselor, I might mention this up front:

> *Mary, I know how much it concerns you that you haven't made many friends since transferring to this school. Let's talk a bit about some ways to make that situation better. In a little while, however, I'd like for you to help me bring in a couple of boxes from my car. Would you help me with that?*

The diversion can be anything really. It actually gives Mary a moment to reflect on options and possibilities rather than feeling "on-the-spot" with the issue. (You might even give her some "think about it" homework as she helps you with the boxes.)

In my training entitled *The Oppositional and Defiant Child*, I tell teachers they have many opportunities for powerful and short interactions of support with students. For instance, a teacher could share the following comments with a student just before class starts (it would take less than 20 seconds):

> *Jimmy, I really love your smile. But your mom told me last night your dog is really sick, and that you're very worried about her. Jimmy, as much as I love your smile, If you don't feel like smiling in my class sometimes—well, it's okay with me. I can handle it."*

This bit of interaction is based on fact and the knowledge of how much the teacher already knows about Jimmy and his dog. There's not much to uncover, only support. The greatest compliment Jimmy could pay his teacher would be to look sad in her class. She gave him a license to be real.

With the teacher or the counselor, there's always an opportunity to check back with the youngster again and again. I'm not inferring that 20 seconds fixes everything.

19

"Paper Sack Therapy?"

(That's right, paper sack therapy)

This intervention is a close cousin to "A Little at a Time, Please," except it offers the benefit of a tangible quality. It is powerful in its simplicity. Although my original thoughts were to use it only with young children, I have discovered it works well with adolescents also.

As you work with a student, have her help you cut pieces of paper into strips on the short side, so that you end up with strips about 1x8" in size. Offer to be her "secretary" by writing on a strip something that could be a concern or a problem for her. These could include issues with home and family, peers, school performance and community involvement. Put only one "problem" on a strip. The idea is to have somewhere between six and a dozen strips. Hand her a manila envelope and ask her to personalize it with her name, artwork, whatever. Put the strips inside the envelope, then say:

> *Julie, as we visit we'll take the last ten minutes of each session to draw a strip from the envelope and look at the concern written on it. We'll discuss how you're doing with that concern or issue. When we draw a strip that is no longer a concern, we'll remove it. Sometimes we might add strips to the envelope.*

I did not originate this intervention, but I like it and I've used it successfully many times. It brings short-term focus to issues without making the child too uncomfortable in the process. The youngster is more apt to validate her concerns knowing the session will be over shortly.

A paper lunch sack can also be used for collecting the slips. Just fold the top down and secure it with a clothes pin. The child can decorate the sack and put it on your bookshelf. My reason for using the manila clasp envelope is that it's a bit more confidential and can be stored out of sight. Young children, however, might *want* to see their sack on your bookshelf. Just reinforce the notion that what's in a sack belongs *only* to the person whose name is on it.

20

"NOBODY Can Make Me Smile!"

(Just watch me.)

Kids should have the freedom to smile or not; their choice. But here's an intervention that is so much fun, you'll just *have* to try it.

The next time you work with a youngster who has trouble smiling, or who simply won't give it a try, make a pair of these big balloon lips. They are made with entertainer's balloons. (They're called "260s," that means when blown up they are two inches in diameter and 60 inches in length.) I used to carry a couple in my pocket all the time.

I model a pair of them, often telling the youngster that I am not going to remove them *until* they smile. It usually works. (One girl asked if I would make her a pair. Then we walked over to the administration building and modeled them for the folks there. (It helps to be a little spontaneous in this business.)

Here are the instructions for making the balloon lips. They are taken from a book I wrote for teachers, *101 Ways to Make Your Classroom Special* (reprinted here with permission).

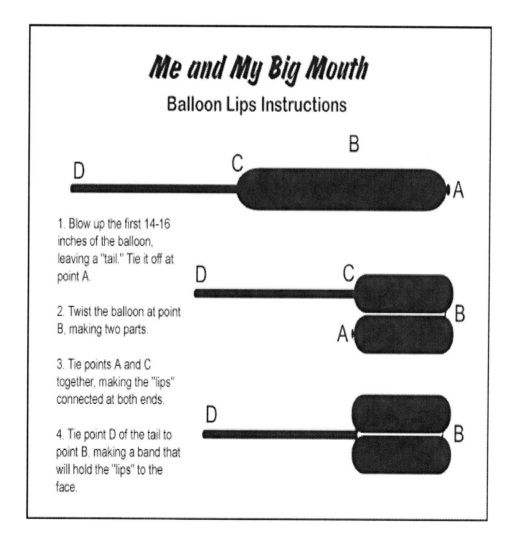

Me and My Big Mouth

Balloon Lips Instructions

1. Blow up the first 14-16 inches of the balloon, leaving a "tail." Tie it off at point A.

2. Twist the balloon at point B, making two parts.

3. Tie points A and C together, making the "lips" connected at both ends.

4. Tie point D of the tail to point B, making a band that will hold the "lips" to the face.

21

"You ARE Whistling DIXIE!

(Like hear it again?)

I was training counselors once at the University of Oklahoma when the discussion got around to ways to capture a youngster's attention. One counselor casually mentioned that she whistles "Dixie" through a soda straw in these situations. Apparently, it always works.

After a demonstration (that was a given, huh?), she noted that, when a straw is in a soft drink, the end in the liquid is sealed off. That means it's like blowing on any small tube that's closed on the bottom. (Of course, we had a "Dixie" contest. Advice: Don't try to whistle and laugh at the same time.)

Idea: You could promise to whistle "Dixie" if the child complies with a request. Try it; it's fun. (And no more ridiculous than wearing a balloon on your face.)

22

"You Didn't Hear What I THOUGHT?"

(Sorry; think it again and I'll listen closer.)

I was walking Elaine over to my office, We crossed the parking lot the school and the Special Education cooperative shared.

Out of the clear blue this fourth grader blurted, "She like the red ones best!"

"Elaine, I guess I don't understand," I said. "What do you mean by telling me someone liked the red ones best?"

She gave me a slightly perturbed glance, took an deep breath, and went into her explanation.

"My mother's in the hospital. Before we went to see her Saturday, we picked some flowers from the front of the house. I got to give them to her. She liked the red ones best. Understand?

Elaine never realized that her first statement was mostly unstated. She thought part of it, said part of it, and thought she said *all* of it.

This could be a clue to anxiety, the sort of anxiety that affects thought and expression, or it could be an indication of more involved difficulty with thought itself. A good psychological assessment could help evaluate the situation and give you more information.

It is for certain that, if a child like Elaine were to make more and more sense as you work with her, you're probably doing her some good.

Students who operate with a high level of anxiety likely will have trouble attending in class and achieving in academics. It wouldn't be at all surprising to discover this child is missing big chunks and pieces of instruction in the classroom. It's all part of the same problem.

Keep in mind that difficult and defiant students can also experience interference with anxiety and thought.

23

"Can I Ask YOU a Question?"

(Fire away!)

If a youngster only answers your questions, that's not interaction—
that's an interview. With one exception, I always value comments from a
youngster that are *not* prompted by me in some way.

Spontaneous, unsolicited interaction from a student can mean some or
all of the following (three are good; one isn't):

1. You have developed rapport with the child.

2. The youngster either has good people skills, or could
learn them quickly.

3. The youngster sees you as a valid resource and wants
to utilize what you have to offer.

4. The student wants to turn up the charm and see if he
can manipulate you in some way (such as a request for a
special favor).

If it is an initial visit with a student, I like to note *when* in the session the
child initiated a spontaneous comment and what it was about. Often, the
comments are conversational and not really "deep," such as, "Do you have
any kids?" At other times a spontaneous question like, "What would *you*
have done in that situation?" could be a genuine search for guidance and
support.

I'm sure we have all been manipulated by youngsters who either want us
to solve all their problems for them (without them doing *anything*), or who
want us to give or allow a special favor. (I saw this a lot when working with

youngsters in juvenile detention. They were always sugar-sweet—until I told them, "No, I won't do that." Then their face and attitude changed dramatically, sometimes salted with an explicative or two.)

24

"You're NOT Supposed to Know the Answers!"

(I only know a few—but WHICH few?)

There's no one hard and fast rule for telling if a youngster is lying to you, but I've developed a little strategy along the way that works pretty well for me.

Before I visit with the youngster, I try to grab a few facts about him and his reported behavior (if any). I try to glean a few choice facts, if possible.

(It's always a toss-up about how much up-front information we should collect on a youngster before seeing the individual. If we collect too much, it might affect our impressions of the child before we even visit with him. If we don't collect enough, we might neglect some questions that need to be asked.)

As I have already mentioned, I have worked with quite a few youngsters (about 90% boys) who were in major trouble with the law. A boy's offense report would contain plenty of information, along with some very specific facts that would only be known to him and the arresting officer. But the youngster *wouldn't* know I had read the report.

In one instance it was a young man who had been caught wandering the streets high on aerosol paint. I asked him for his version of what happened and, true to form, his account of the facts of the situation were very close to

37

the officer's account in the report. (Most kids, once caught, will share the *facts* of the situation, but not the *responsibility* for them. This usually comes out ringing loud and clear in an assessment.)

If he answered my next question correctly, I felt I could put some validity into how he would respond to questions for which I had no outside answers.

"What color was the paint," I asked.

"Silver." The color fit with the officer's report.

This questioning approach is quite flexible to a lot of situations. Having just a little information the student would never suspect you knew can offer you leverage for assessing how truthful the youngster is regarding other things.

25

"That's NOT Funny!"

(I thought it WAS funny.)

Some youngsters, especially those who are emotionally rigid and fragile, tend to exhibit one-way humor. They don't mind a good joke, so long as it is on someone else. If the joke is on them, they can become very angry and upset.

The assessment of their capacity to take a joke on themselves is something I call *The Humor Test*. It offers a relatively decent measure of flexibility of affect. After all, when we can laugh at ourselves, we can become more tolerant of a *lot* of things.

In practice, this is not something I do "on demand," because that would *not* be spontaneous. But I do look for opportunities to take a friendly "jab" at the youngster so I can see how she handles it.

Such an opportunity came with one 17-year-old girl as she came into the building following a fight on the steps with her boyfriend. She was still fuming as she came through the door carrying her books. She saw me.

"Looks like you and John aren't exactly ready to go out and pick out the furniture," I said.

She glared at me and picked out a book with her right hand. She cocked back her arm, preparing to throw it straight at my head. I was ready to duck.

As she drew back there was a glimmer of a smile. She paused, then smiled broadly, put the book down and came into my office.

That one worked. Although most youngsters and adults don't *like* being the object of a joke, they can usually absorb it without much trouble. Youngsters who become extremely angry and enraged are so delicate emotionally I would wonder about their capacity to handle even minor difficulties. There's no room for error in their tolerance for frustration.

26

"Oh, a Four, I Guess—Maybe a Five."

(Thanks, that helps me.)

Youngsters don't have to describe their emotional state in order for a counselor to understand it. This notion is especially important if the counselor wishes to know if the child herself is recognizing any progress.

The solution is a simple scale. The youngster doesn't have to flounder for words to describe her feelings about anger, for instance. She only has to give you a number. Here's a scale for anger:

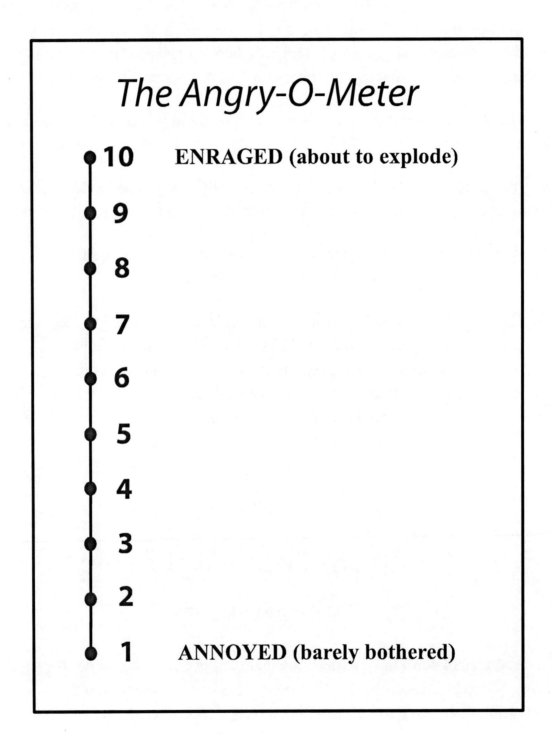

The Angry-O-Meter

10   **ENRAGED (about to explode)**

9

8

7

6

5

4

3

2

1   **ANNOYED (barely bothered)**

A scale like this has a huge advantage over descriptive terms that can be confusing, like "upset," "angry," "mad," and "livid." All the child has to give you is a number. (It's good, of course, if the numbers go *down* as you work with the child.)

Print the scale on half-sheets of paper (two up). Ask the youngster to circle the number that represents where she is at the moment. (This could be anger in general, or anger regarding specific issues.) Ask her to sign and date the sheets (or you can do it for them, including the specific issue, if there is one), then save it with the others. It can be good to go back and show a child where she once was in her anger. It shows progress and lends to the child a sense of improvement and more control.

27

"Can We Do This with OTHER Feelings?"

(Absolutely!)

The scaling of anger is only the beginning. The concept works very well for depression (Sad-O-Meter), worry (Worry-O-Meter), anxiety (Tense-O-Meter) and other feelings, including good ones (Happy-O-Meter). Let me share a short story that shows just how valuable this notion of scaling can be.

I was working with a 10-year-old girl who lived in a group home. (Her mother had severe health issues and couldn't take care of her.) Her houseparents were concerned about her; she seemed "weepy" much of the time at home. I was thinking of a referral for possible medication, but on the other hand, it could have been a normal phase through which she would pass. I decided to visit with her and use the scale strategy.

I explained to her the concerns of her houseparents. She acknowledged their concern and shared she had been having some difficulty. When I asked her to put her sadness on a scale from one to ten, she replied, "Oh, a two, maybe a three."

Her response told me that she was handling it, and that she did not see her sadness (depression) as being anything overwhelming. Likewise, her grades and relationships were holding at school. I spoke with her houseparents and her caseworker; we decided to wait.

It was a good decision. In another week or two the "weepy" symptoms all but disappeared. Her "old self" returned on its own.

28

"I LIKE Being Covered in Pillows"

(Really?)

One facility where I saw youngsters for counseling had a very large waiting room outside my inner office. Because it was roomier and frankly more comfortable for the youngsters I saw, much of my work with them was done in the waiting room (when I knew it was going to be empty).

A high school girl came for a session, a first visit. She sat on the large couch as far from me as she could get. As we visited, she took all the throw pillows and piled them around herself.

With a smile, I commented about the pillows: "Looks like you're building a barricade to protect yourself. Am I *that* scary?"

She laughed and denied the barricade notion, but the pillows *stayed* right where they were.

"Oh, it's not a big deal to me," I shared. "I think all of us subconsciously look for ways to 'protect' ourselves in situations where we might feel a little uncomfortable. But pillows are better than a chain-link fence, huh?"

I asked her if she'd like to help me with something (probably the old "boxes in my car" thing), which she was eager to do. We left the waiting room. As the session was closing we came back.

She sat down on the couch, not quite as far from me as earlier. She reached for the pillows, then stopped. She didn't barricade with them, and she never did again.

Obviously the pillows were never the issue; recognizing discomfort and dealing with it *was* the issue. Perhaps even more important is the skill of *not* transmitting one's vulnerabilities any more than necessary.

I've used the same intervention with youngsters who sat with their arms crossed through a session, or showed some other defensive postures. They aren't bad, but worth noting at some point. It's a sure sign of developing rapport when these defensive postures cease.

29

"Okay; I'll Answer ONE Easy Question!"

(Sounds fair to me.)

Some youngsters are genuinely afraid to talk about things that trouble them. They are afraid that, if they talk about their problems, the problems become even *bigger*. They're also afraid that, if they ever *begin* to express emotions, they won't be able to contain them, or that a problem will somehow get out of its box and do serious damage somehow.

For some youngsters it's even more than fear; it borders on outright panic. One way to set a child more at ease and still focus on a valid issue is to use a strategy I call *The One Question Limit*. It works like this:

> *Suzanne, it seems to me that there are some things that are very hard for you to talk about. I understand that. What I'd like to do is ask you just one question, a question you can answer "Yes" or "No." Regardless of how you answer my "Yes" or "No" question, I promise you I won't ask you any more questions about that subject TODAY. Do you understand, Suzanne? May I ask you the one "Yes" or "No" question?*

She indicated that one question would be fine. (I've *never* had a youngster refuse. I think it's because one "Yes" or "No" question is reasonable; refusing a "Yes" or "No" questions would *not* be reasonable. The operative word in the statement to Suzanne, however, is *today*. There was no promise that an issue would *never* be discussed.)

> *Okay then, here's my question. Suzanne, when you learned that your mother and father were getting a divorce, did it bother you? I don't mean like a little, I mean did it bother you—a LOT?*

That's just about as painless as you can ask a painful question. When she nodded "Yes," Suzanne was actually answering TWO questions: the divorce bothered her and it bothered her a lot.

This intervention actually sets up your next visit with Suzanne, when you can ask her, "When you told me that it bothered you a lot, what about your folks getting a divorce bothers you the most?"

30

"He Would NEVER Do That!"

(Careful, NEVER is a long time.)

Adolescents can become pretty rigid when they want to lock out all possibility of being disappointed. (I suppose younger kids can be rigid also, but adolescents take the prize.) Rigid thinking, however, can set a child up for disappointment.

I was working once with a girl who lived in a wonderful group home in south Texas. Her father, the only parent that could be located, placed her in the home because much of his time was spent on an offshore drilling rig in the Gulf of Mexico. Her caseworker, the administrator in charge of the cottages and I weren't at all sure if Dad could be counted on to stay in touch with his daughter. After all his promises to the home and to her, he failed to show up to take her home for her first weekend visit.

She was devastated. But, as you might guess, he renewed all his promises by phone, vowing never to let her down again.

As the weekend approached for his promised visit, I tried to prepare her for what *could* happen. She completely dismissed it. The fact that she might be stood up again wasn't even something she'd talk about.

I tried to explain to her that I wasn't inferring that her father was a bad person. I just meant it wouldn't be a bad idea for her to have a backup plan.

"How sure are you about this," I asked.

"Very sure. I'm *positive* he'll be here Friday afternoon to take me home for the weekend."

I reached into my desk drawer an pulled out a small index card.

"That's two days away; anything could happen. I mean your dad's car could break down on the way out here. But you seem so certain. Are you willing to put it in writing?" I held out the card.

She snatched it out of my hand and, brimming with confidence, wrote "My father will be here to pick me up this Friday." She signed and dated it and passed it back to me.

"I sincerely hope you are right," I told her, then I held up the card. "But if he doesn't come, would you agree that this could be your way of telling yourself you need to be better prepared *next* time?"

She agreed and, as I had suspected, Dad didn't show.

Young people *should* be able to count on promises made to them by family members. Unfortunately, some of those promises stay pretty empty.

31

"Come On; That's NOT Fair!"

(Maybe, but it keeps us talking.)

Dr. Doug Riley, author of *The Defiant Child*, discusses the frustration of asking a child a "Why?" question, only to have the youngster stare at you in silence. For theses situations, he uses an intervention he calls *Splitting the Universe*. Basically it amounts to offering a child a *much* smaller menu.

An "either/or" menu couldn't get much smaller, could it? A very limited menu is a source of frustration for a difficult or defiant youngster because it causes them to either select from the menu (not difficult) or expose more of their defiance than they care to show. "I don't know" just won't work with an "either/or" menu without it looking like, "I don't want to answer your stupid question!"

The menu can even be confrontive, as it probably will be with a difficult or defiant student. "When you were told to come to my office, did you think it might have something to do with the trouble you're having in Mrs. Reagan's class, or did you think I was going down a list of students and pulled your name at random?"

You might get some stalling, because the student can see what's coming. If he stalls too long, simply say, "I'll tell you this much. One of those reasons is true. Which one?"

Splitting the Universe is also great to use to get a youngster on the right track (usually a track with some *responsibility* on it). "When Tommy gave you a mean look and walked away, did you think you had done something to upset him, or did you think he was just having a bad day?"

It's a great tool.

32

"Hey, You're Playing MY Game Now!"

(Yes, I KNOW!)

When a difficult or defiant child or adolescent give you the silent treatment following your question, he might just be waiting for *you* to break the silence.

If you can stand it, just wait it out. (That's hard to do because, as helping professionals, we are very verbal; silence doesn't seem like a good thing at all.) Consider that, just perhaps, the best stuff is happening in the silence. The longer a child remains silent (assuming his resistance is deliberate), the more he has to expose his defiance. At some point he gets pretty uncomfortable, especially if you don't interrupt the silence.

If you do have to interrupt the silence, say something like:

> *You know, that is a tough question. I'll give you all the time you need on it. I have some things to work on here; just let me know when you have an answer. It's not a problem. Take all the time you need. I'll be here until 8:00 P.M. or so tonight.*

When I used to do a lot of assessments, I'd close by telling the child that, since I had asked him a bunch of questions, he could ask me any question he wanted. Then I would *wait* on the answer. Some of those questions were *very* interesting.

33

"Can We Just Get Out of HERE?"

(My thoughts exactly.)

The counselor's office is a semi-intimidating place for some youngsters. They don't always do their best thinking there.

There's nothing wrong with a change of scenery. One of my best sessions ever was with the "weepy" girl mentioned earlier. She was showing a lamb at the junior stock show and offered to show me the animal. We later walked a short distance to a rail fence and admired the open spaces as we visited. She did more reflecting with me in those few moments than a dozen sessions before.

I've visited with youngsters at picnic tables, on a swing set, on a basketball court, in a shop with tools and on a brisk nature walk. All those sessions were quite productive.

These options are more limited in a school environment, both logistically and from a standpoint of confidentiality. But a little creativity can pay off in a big way.

34

"Would You HELP Me With Something?"

(Sure, what can I do for you.)

It's a compliment to your developing relationship with a youngster when she asks you to help her with something. This means she sees you as a valued resource, not just another adult at school.

My personal experience has been that the request for help has little or nothing to do with what is discussed in counseling, but rather represents the youngster's desire to extend the relationship in some way. Of course, she might really need some help with something.

One of my counseling cases, a high school girl, stopped me one day. She was writing a paper about the Vietnam War and needed to interview a Vietnam veteran. The problem was she didn't know any, until someone mentioned to her that I had served in Vietnam. She asked if she could interview me and we set a time to meet for the interview.

She had another problem. She wanted to scan some pictures of the Vietnam War Memorial (the "Wall") and put them into her report, but she couldn't find any. I just happened to have an expiring Vietnam War Memorial calendar in my office; it had lots of very good and touching photos. When I gave it to her, you would have thought she had just won the lottery.

For months, that young lady thanked me for the interview and that calendar. She told me she had earned an "A" on that report.

35

"Are You REALLY That Dumb?"

(I'll never tell.)

There are lots of ways to develop rapport with a child on a first visit, but one of my favorites involves origami. I fold a bird (crane) while I talk with the child. (Part of my reason for doing this is that eye contact is not a problem; the child's eyes are on the paper I'm folding.)

I keep up a verbal patter as I fold slowly. I stop abruptly, then look at the child with a confused look on my face (*not* difficult).

"What am I making," I ask. "I forgot."

"A bird."

"Oh, yeah, that's right." I continue on for a bit, then do it again.

"Oh, no! I forgot again. What am I making?"

"It's a *bird*," the child says, with a giggle or two thrown in.

Of course I do this several more times before I actually finish the crane. Kids get to laughing and absolutely love it, although one young student did ask me once, "Are you *really* that dumb?

By the way, if you try this intervention, it's fine to give the finished bird to the child, but you might want to have the student pick it up when school it out. Otherwise, you'll get several dozen requests before the day is over.

36

"Show Me the MONEY!"

(Keep your shirt on.)

I learned to do origami while stationed in Japan. I got pretty good at it. I even learned some of the more complicated designs. It's a lot of fun and something you can do spontaneously just about anywhere with only a piece

of paper. It captures the attention of young people and opens conversation.

A few years back, I ran across a website on making origami items out of paper money. I made several of the items, including this shirt. It's a bit more difficult because a dollar bill isn't square, but there's something about it being MONEY that gets a kid's attention. (Kids? Adults like this just as much!)

There's a man named Clay Randall; you can find him on a "money origami" Google or Yahoo search. He has a site that shows you how to make all kinds of things out of paper money. It's well worth a look.

37

"I Can be Angry and NOT Get in Trouble?"

(Yes, if you do it the right way.)

Teach the youngster the "secret" skill of noncoercive response. "Noncoercive" seems to be a buzz word today in the research literature. And it should be; it connect with the old adage, "Keep your head while those around you are losing theirs" (or something like that).

Most conflicts involve coercive elements. It's rarely the issue that starts the conflict that creates so much trouble as much as it is the interaction within the conflict itself. Consider this scenario, which shows you it's not just children who have trouble with coercive elements:

Wife to husband: *Why are you so HATEFUL all the time?*

Husband's response: *ANYONE married to YOU would become hateful sooner or later.*

Does anyone seriously think that this discussion will get any better? People have been shot *dead* over these kinds of conflicts.

Within the school environment there are always those youngsters who are quite good at pushing the buttons of other students. And, of course, there are those students who accommodate them, who walk around holding out their button box. One's a match; the other's a strip of sandpaper.

You see it every single day.

One solution to the coercive process (arguments that escalate), is simply for one of the two in the conflict to shut down the coercion. It's not something that is guaranteed to work every time, nor are all personality styles receptive to it, but it generally gives the person who *implements* the solution control over the immediate circumstances and the outcomes. And, if the outcomes are positive, there is strong reinforcement to make this intervention work again and again. (A lot of folks have done work on the notion of noncoercive response, but I especially like the work of Israel Kalman, a psychotherapist from Staten Island, New York.) Here's a model of the intervention process:

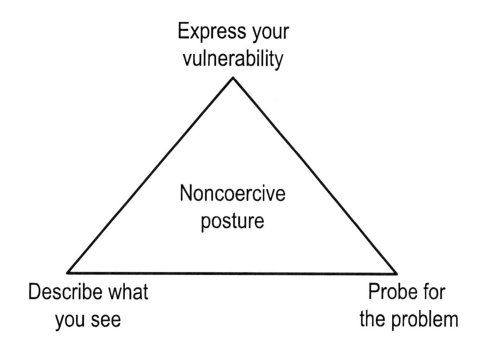

As you can see, the central part of the process is for one to maintain a noncoercive posture throughout the conflict. This is *not* easy, but critical. Then the person working the model acknowledges that the other person is upset, expresses the fact that they *don't* like what's happening (a very honest perspective), then probes for whatever the *real* problem might be.

As mentioned earlier, it's not a perfect intervention but, when it works, it is very empowering.

Let's consider an example. Imagine that you've been working with Jimmy on this noncoercive intervention to provocation. Later in the day, Marty, one of Jimmy's friends, calls him an "idiot." Using the intervention, Jimmy's response could go something like this:

> *Marty, you just called me an idiot, didn't you? I don't know why you would say something like that to me, but it looks like you are pretty upset about SOMETHING I must have done? I really don't like being called an idiot. What's the problem, Marty? Why would you say that?*

This dialog has all the correct elements in the right order. Although it sounds unlikely that a youngster would actually use this process in a conflict, don't sell Jimmy short. With practice, he can get good at it.

So let him practice. Pair Jimmy up with other students and let them take turns trying the intervention. Just be aware of three potential drawbacks to using this approach:

1. It is a highly verbal intervention. Don't expect students with poor skills of verbal expression to do well with it.

2. It's not for young students who don't have the maturity to conceptualize the process.

3. It won't work at all if the other youngster *doesn't care* about resolving the conflict.

It's also possible for a counselor to use this intervention with a difficult and defiant student who is resistant to counseling. Here's an example of how a counselor might use noncoercive intervention with a student who has just said, "Counseling is STUPID!" (How's that for an attack on you and the whole profession in just three words?)

> *Sarah, I'm not sure I know why you said that, but it looks like you are pretty upset. There must be some reason why you said it. I do know I worked pretty hard to become a counselor, so I really don't care for anyone calling it stupid. What is the problem, Sarah. How can we work this out? I really want to know.*

Noncoercive intervention is a great skill to teach in groups.

38

"You Really DO Care About Me!"

(I certainly do.)

I believe the best things that happen between a youngster and a counselor can occur "unofficially," when they are *not* in a session. This is especially true with the development of rapport early on.

This is best accomplished through what I call *Magic Moments*. These are opportunities the counselor takes to communicate with the student casually on something that is of interest to the youngster. It can be about sports, hobbies, vacations, pets, anything.

These interactions have a spontaneous quality, and though they might not last more that 30-60 seconds, they focus 100% on the youngster and his interests. A good counselor listens carefully, gathering more "material" for the next *Magic Moment* (a trip he'll be taking on the next three-day weekend, a game his team will be playing later this week, or perhaps a new baseball card he's added to his collection).

The power of these very brief but pleasant interactions is that it positions the counselor very favorably in the eyes of the student. (It also works well for teachers.) The youngster is clear on the fact that this is something you *choose* to do, not something you *have* to do.

How do you know when these efforts are beginning to pay off in rapport and trust? You'll know it when the youngster begins to strike up a conversation *first* as you approach her, or when she comes across three aisles in the grocery store just to say hello to you.

Obviously, this intervention should come naturally. If it is contrived, a child will figure it out quickly.

Try this one. It's one of the easiest things to do, but it pays great dividends.

39

"Like a BIG Boy?"

(Like a VERY big boy!)

Counseling with small children means combining activities with our "meaty" objectives of counseling, whatever those might be. It's a given that young ones (and sometimes older ones also), aren't exactly candidates for eyeball-to-eyeball verbal interaction for an hour. If we ever did try that, we might not get them to come back.

At least once in awhile we don't need to *do* something with a young child in order to have a valuable session. The youngster might even welcome the change.

One day Markie came into my office. (There's a hint; he was too young to be called Mark.)

Markie walked straight over to my bookshelf and hauled out a bucket of those little plastic building blocks. Before I could redirect him (I had been on the phone), he dumps the whole thing on the floor.

"I guess therapy has started," I mumbled to myself as I interacted with Markie and helped him create an exact reproduction of The Critter That Ate Manhattan. It didn't take long, not when one of us is five years old.

"You know what, Markie?"

"What?"

"I'd like for you to sit in that chair right there and let me talk to you like a BIG boy."

"Okay." He did, and we did. (I believe my statement, "like a BIG boy," helped.) It was a great visit, and it encouraged me to find "windows" in counseling to wean young ones from the need to always be coloring, building or playing for a whole session.

40

"You're Silly, but I LIKE It!"

(Are you SURE you're not married?)

Years ago, when I did a lot of assessment, I got into the habit of asking young children if they were married. I would do this immediately upon introducing myself. It's a question that develops rapport and gets discussion going quickly. But I primarily ask this question, "Are you married?" in order to assess two important things:

1. I want to see if the child is alert, paying attention to the question. (Some children will nod their head to *any* question you ask them.) Youngsters with a lot of emotional baggage are not alert.

2. Since the question is so ridiculous, I also want to see if an alert child will sense the humor in it. Ideally, a youngster will laugh as they say something like, "I'm NOT married; I'm only six years old." (A youngster with a flat affect won't pick up on the humor, a significant observation.)

"ARE YOU MARRIED ?!"

58

Most kids will figure out I'm just being silly with them, but they like it. It's not at all unusual for a youngster to walk up to me again several days later and say, "And I'm *still* not married!"

The great thing about "Are you married?" is that you can use it again and again by only changing it a bit:

Did I ever ask you if you were married?

I heard you got married over the weekend. Is that true?

What did you tell me your husband's (or wife's) name was?

This rather "different" approach tends to disarm difficult or defiant youngsters. It's something they *don't* expect.

41

"I Brought My LIST!"

(I can see that.)

Earlier we discussed the problem of getting youngsters to identify issues they need to work on in counseling. It's also possible to have the exact *opposite* problem—students who want to personally customize all of the counseling session themselves.

I've had youngsters literally bring a list with them to counseling, a list of issues and items they wanted me to cover. If this were to happen only occasionally, with a student writing down a few things during the week she didn't want to forget, that would be fine, but a list could be a problem for several reasons:

1. The list might contain too many petty gripes and complaints she wants *me* to fix or repair, rather than dealing with them herself. If I became too involved in her list, it could make me more of her personal policeman than her counselor.

2. The list could be a diversion, a focus away from things that might be too difficult or uncomfortable for her to talk about. As long as she can make a list, and as long as I deal with her list items, she's controlling the session and not really improving.

3. Lists can have histrionic characteristics and cause concern about the possibility of emerging borderline features. This is not really a concern with young students, but it is on my mind with adolescents, especially girls.

I worked with one adolescent who brought lists and letters to counseling. She even decorated a binder and gave it to me for storing all the paper she was bringing! This girl brought me the ultimate list, a list of ways to kill herself. She expected me to circle one of them and hand it back to her—a "recommendation," so to speak. Although she was not the typical counseling case, she ended up doing very well. I'm not sure whether she is one of my success stories, or if I was one of her's, but she's happily married today and has five great kids.

42

"My Stepfather's a Jerk!"

(How am I supposed to respond to that?)

He probably *is* a jerk, but you have to be careful how you respond to such a statement, right? If you agree with her, she starts telling her friends and the rest of the world that even her *counselor* says her stepfather is a jerk. About all you need is for some "friendly" confrontation from him. (This stuff *does* have a way of getting around.)

Her statement about her stepdad being a jerk can be a bear trap. Avoid it. The real issue is not his jerk status so much as what is going on between them that's causing the trouble and, more specifically, how she might be able to handle it better. Even then, you're working on only one end of the problem. Our work is difficult enough without hanging out a shingle that reads: ***STEPPARENT REPAIR***.

I had the opportunity to work with a young adolescent at a residential treatment facility. She was doing well in the program. In fact, she was doing so well she earned the opportunity to go home for the weekend.

To her surprise, her mother did not come to pick her up; Mom sent her husband, the girl's stepfather. As soon as she saw him, she ducked into the ladies' rest room and locked the door.

I was talking to her through the door, trying to soothe her enough to go with him.

"No way!" she sobbed. "I'll get into the truck with him and in five minutes we'll be fighting and screaming at each other."

"I know you want to have a good home visit. What if I talk to him and tell him you want the both of you to work really hard on making this a good visit?"

She agreed. When I explained to him the situation, her concern, and how she wanted them both to work on making it a good visit, he lost it right there in the lobby:

> *Yeah, that's just what she wants me to do. Well, I've got a news flash for her. I'm not playing any of her silly, stupid games. You tell her to get her butt out here RIGHT NOW. I'm already running late.*

She didn't go. Smart girl. We weren't able to "fix" her family, but we did insist that Mom pick her up from then on. And, as I remember, the girl did very well in treatment.

43

"You Want to Learn About ME?"

(If you'll help me.)

The direct approach might be the best one to take with the youngster who is especially cautious in visiting with you. It works well in an interview-type format where you're collecting information. This direct approach begins with a sincere expression and a statement something like this:

Scott, it's my job this morning to learn as much as I can about you, if you will help me. Then I can better determine the things we can do here at school that will work out best for you. Will you help me? Will you help me learn as much as I can about YOU?

I don't believe it's possible to be any *more* direct than that. It's not only an appeal to the child for help (and most kids are willing to help) the object of all that help is an important person—*them.*

It's interesting, isn't it, how we can create technology that does amazing things, but one amazing way to connect with another human being is to ask them to help us. That's a skill that hasn't changed in six thousand years.

44

"Nope; NEVER!"

(It's 100% your choice.)

Forgiveness cannot be mandated. My pet peeve is the counselor who tells a youngster (or an adult, for that matter) she will never get better until she forgives the one who has hurt her. Although I happen to agree that forgiveness is an important, even critical, component for achieving healing, to stress it as a *requirement* might only add to the hurt.

Why would we want to create more hurt? It doesn't make sense.

Authentic forgiveness requires at least five awarenesses:

    1. An awareness that there was damage done

    2. An awareness of what forgiveness is

3. An awareness of a need to forgive

4. An awareness of how to forgive

5. An awareness to let what is forgiven stay forgiven

It takes time and some work to make sure the youngster has these awarenesses in place, or is ready to work on getting them into place.

For someone to exercise forgiveness, she must be in touch with the hurt the forgiveness is about. If a counselor tries to discuss forgiveness while the youngster is still needing the "insulation" her anger provides, it just won't work. She's not ready, as evidenced by reluctance to even discuss forgiveness, let alone exercise it.

Patience can pay off here. I've worked with youngsters who said they would *never* forgive, only to exercise it a few weeks later. With kids especially, "never" can be just around the corner.

The ability to exercise actual forgiveness involves someone asking for it. How often is that *really* going to happen? With some youngsters and their family dynamics, those opportunities are rare indeed. Within therapeutic settings, I've seen it only a handful of times.

But there's a way to help the youngster without her having to play the waiting game forever. She can exercise what I call *The Spirit of Forgiveness*. It's a youngster's active decision about what she would do *if* she were asked to forgive. A counselor might set it up like this:

> *Sally, if _____ were to ever come to you and say that he was wrong in how he treated you and asked for your forgiveness, and if you KNEW he was sincere, what would you do?*

64

You'll get one of three answers:

1. "I would forgive him."

2. "I would *not* forgive him."

3. "He'd never ask me that" or "Sincere? That would never happen."

The third option is typical of what you'll get from difficult and defiant youngsters or the child who is hesitant to consider forgiveness. I would want to push for a "Yes" or a "No," so I "qualify" the asker's sincerity by asking the youngster if there is someone in her life who would *always* tell her the truth and would *never* lie to her. The child can do that (it's often a grandparent). Then I would say:

> *If your grandmother told you that she knew for certain he was deeply sorry for the way he had treated you and was very sincere in asking for your forgiveness, what would you do?*

If the youngster says that, under those circumstances, she probably would forgive him, you can tell her she's now completed the hard work. No only has she exercised the *willingness* to forgive, in spirit she has *accomplished* forgiveness, whether she's ever asked or not.

Although I can attest to the fact that this intervention *does* work, I've also experiences situations where youngsters will slip back into unforgiveness. Although I'm far from having all the answers here, I believe one of the reasons for such a "slip" is that it hurts less to be angry than it hurts to be vulnerable. Forgiveness requires vulnerability.

This intervention works well in group counseling because a youngster can utilize the experiences, support and feedback of peers. This is very powerful stuff.

45

"That's a TOUGH Decision!"

(It certainly is.)

After a youngster forgives or exercises *The Spirit of Forgiveness*, there's one more therapeutic piece of business: she must make a decision about how the future relationship will be with that person.

Sometimes youngsters erroneously believe they must make major concessions in a relationship as a result of their forgiveness. That's not true. It's possible for a youngster to forgive someone and still not choose to be around them very much.

But if a youngster makes a conscious effort to avoid someone they have forgiven, how does that look? If she's not careful, she can make the original offender look like *her* victim. That's why a decision about the relationship is important.

I have found that young people think about this relationship only in the short-term. They don't think far enough out, especially if the person is going to be a figure in her life for several decades. One adolescent girl hung a pretty good frame on the future relationship with her stepfather (she had forgiven him for being mean to her) when she said:

> *For MY sake, I really don't want to be around him much.*
> *But one of days I'll be married and will have children.*
> *He'll be the grandpa on that side of the family. If I avoid*
> *him too much, it might not be good for my kids. So I'll do*
> *the right thing. We'll go over to the house for Christmas*
> *Dinner and to open presents, but we're not staying over.*

That's a pretty mature perspective, isn't it? My guess is she will find the right combination of approach and withdrawal that will be comfortable for her.

Stress that the youngster come to decisions about how the relationship will be in the future. A lot will depend on those decisions.

46

"Will ACCEPTANCE Work Instead?"

(Yes, if it's the best you can do right now.)

It's difficult, bordering on impossible, to be 100% in touch with another person's pain. We always run their accounts and their experiences through our own filters. "That wouldn't bother me, so why should it bother him," we might think.

We could be wrong, so to suggest that youngsters consider forgiveness might be to suggest something they *cannot* do. Either their view or perspective on the hurt done them is affected, or the damage done them is something they cannot forgive. Either way, attempting to forgive would be liking taking a trip in the sand. Youngsters would become bogged down to the point that all their effort would go in one direction—deeper into the hole.

Perhaps a youngster can't forgive, but he still desires to move through and past the pain. What does he do?

Here's where acceptance is an option. Acceptance acknowledges the hurt and its consequences, but without the intervention of forgiveness. Acceptance essentially says, "It happened, but I choose not to keep dwelling on it. I'll put it in the past and move on."

47

"You Just Going to STAND There?"

(Shhh; I'm thinking.)

We know there are youngsters who relate better to the counselor when they are *doing* something (as opposed to simply sitting and visiting). Unfortunately, the "doing something" can become a distraction in itself (such as the sportsmanship of a game of chess overpowering the therapeutic value of the session). It happens all the time; it can become a concern, especially when the child sees counseling sessions as "game time."

Here's a strategy that works for me. At one facility where I worked, we had a nice pool table in a back room. (I did some of my best work around that pool table.) I'd offer to play some pool with a youngster, provided he would continue to visit with me in the process. (Youngsters *always* agree, but later become a little too absorbed in the logistics of the game.)

Well, if it's my turn, the kid knows he can't take a shot until I do, right? Here's where I would slow it down by posing a question and *waiting* on the answer. I'd start to take a shot, then stop and look up at the boy with a confused, questioning look on my face:

Tommy, I just now was wondering what you might have been thinking when your stepmom said that to you. Do you think she was angry at you, or was she actually angry at your father?

Then I *don't* take a shot until he answers. Very effective. By the way, did you notice my *Splitting the Universe* strategy in my question to Tommy? Had I said, "What do you believe she was thinking, Tommy?" he would probably have said, "I don't know." I gave him a simple menu and waited on a response.

48

"Wow! I Get to Work on YOU?"

(Yeah; It's Been a LONG Day.)

The "secret" to working with difficult and defiant youngsters is to take them *out* of their comfort zone. As discussed earlier, this can mean finding creative ways of being unpredictable.

Try role reversal as an intervention. Point them to your chair, then sit where they would sit. (I had a short couch in one of my offices. I'd flop down on it, as if I was too exhausted to do much else—which was sometimes true.)

"I've had a long and rigorous day," you might say. "Why don't you be *my* counselor today?"

Here's your golden opportunity to show oppositional and defiant youngsters what's it's like to be on the receiving end of their aggravation.

Well, what do you want me to say?

Hey, YOU'RE the counselor. I'd like for you to say that we could both go home early, but that would get you fired.

So what do I do if I'M supposed to be the counselor?

Okay, let's suppose that my big brother just got shipped out to Iraq. My mother has told you that I am very worried about him—so worried I'm having nightmares. But I won't talk about it to ANYONE! Get me to talk about it.

How do I do THAT?

Hey, YOU'RE the counselor!

That's enough dialog. See where I'm going with it? Here's a youngster who is beginning to find out that a counselor's job *isn't* that easy.

It's actually possible to cover some quality ground in this mode because you're not only the "kid" being counseled in this scenario, you're actually giving him tips on how he could tap into the feelings of another person and attempt to help them. That's a good skill, and it includes material you can use later.

Another benefit of occasional role reversal is that, whenever this youngster starts to be difficult with you in the future, you can kindly remind him of what it felt like to be on the other end of that defiant behavior.

Occasional role reversal can be a great break in the scheme of things and, as mentioned, it can actually be helpful to the purpose of counseling. If you try role reversal as an intervention strategy, you will find the youngster gets better and better at it.

49

"This Mitt Looks DUMB!"

(Then take it off.)

Anger is a very *good* thing. It acknowledges an attack on one's needs. Anger moves one to action (sometimes *too much* action).

Staying angry, on the other hand, is a problem, especially if goes on and on and on. But, since anger "covers" our vulnerable feelings, like embarrassment, failure and humiliation, it hurts less to stay angry.

So that's what a lot of folks do. They stay angry, but at the cost of staying insulated from the good as well as the bad. They wear their anger like they would wear a blanket of insulation, and they never take it off. These are *not* happy people.

Here's a story that explains how anger works, and why it isn't intended to be a permanent thing.

> *Susan goes to the stove to take a pot off the burner. But when she touches the handle of the pot, it burns her. Her hand hurts. It hurts a LOT! Susan finds a big oven mitt in the kitchen. It's perfect. She puts the big oven mitt on her hand so she doesn't get burned again.*

Susan DOESN'T get burned again, so she keeps the mitt on. Even when her mother tells Susan to move all the pots from the pantry to the bottom drawer in the kitchen, she keeps the mitt on.

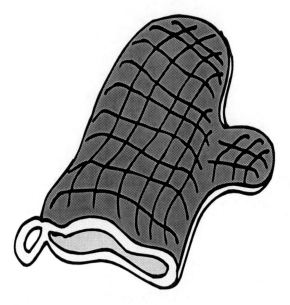

Those pots aren't even hot, but no matter. She keeps the mitt on. Susan doesn't want to EVER get burned again. She keeps the mitt on when she sweeps the floor, when she does her homework, and when she goes to bed. She even wears the mitt to school the next day. Susan doesn't want to get burned again.

Susan meets a new student at school and shakes her hand, with an oven mitt on her own hand. The new student thinks Susan is a little strange. Her friends try to get her to take off the mitt.

But Susan's scared. She might be burned again.

What should Susan do?

Obviously, if I'm working with a boy, the child's name in the story becomes Sam. The story has two-way application: to take off a mitt (anger) that no longer serves its purpose, and to make a decision to deal with more situations bare-handed rather than search for a mitt.

As good an intervention as this one is with a single child, it works even better in the group counseling setting. It's also a great intervention to use when talking about anger in the classroom environment.

Our need to experience vulnerability (and pain) was perhaps best expressed by Anne Morrow Lindbergh, prize-winning author and the wife of the famous aviator, Charles Lindbergh. The painful experience she references was the kidnapping and murder of their first child (thus the famous Lindbergh Trial of the '30s):

> *In the end one has to discard shields and remain open and vulnerable. Otherwise, scar tissue will seal off the wound and no growth will follow. To grow, to be reborn, one must remain vulnerable—open to love, but also hideously open to the possibility of more suffering.*

It can't be said any better than that. It's no coincidence that Anne Lindbergh lived to be almost 95. Vulnerability can be a good thing.

50

"I'm not as ANGRY anymore?"

(What does that mean?)

It is possible for a youngster to deal pretty well with his anger and frustration, but not really see much of the improvement.

We can tell him, but it's better if *he* tells him.

Since youngsters don't always see gradual change, it's helpful to compare how they are doing with how they used to be in those areas and issues that were difficult for them. This could be a sample dialog. The counselor speaks first:

John, how are you doing in controlling your anger now?

I don't know; I'm not sure.

Still getting in trouble and going to the office a couple times a week?

No, I haven't been to the office in three weeks.

Still arguing with your teachers and doing poorly in your grades.

No, I'm better there. Right now I'm passing.

Is your girlfriend still trying to break up with you?

No, we're okay now.

Hmmm, not getting sent to the office much anymore, getting along better with your teachers, passing in your classes and you and your girlfriend are good. What do you think all that means?

That I getting better and I'm learning how to handle my anger?

Sure sounds like it to me.

I sometimes think young people are looking for some kind of Hocus-Pocus mystical spell that's going to come over them and make them into some kind of compliant zombie. By far, the easiest way to convince them of their improvement is to reflect not so much on what is happening, but by what is *not* happening. Then we let them interpret it.

It amounts to building mental health brick by brick.

51

"THIS Rock, THAT window?"

(Hey, do what you gotta do.)

We always have more control that we *think* we do. The new soldier in battle is afraid he will cut and run when the battle gets tough. But he doesn't.

Young people sometimes feel their behavior is somehow out of their control, that something is making them or driving them to act out inappropriately. The danger with this "The Devil Made Me Do It!" thinking is that it removes any sense of responsibility for one's actions.

(There are serious medical and psychological conditions whereby individuals experience serious disruptions and distortions of thought. These folks are *not* the focus of what we're talking about here.)

When Dr. Doug Riley, child and adolescent psychologist and author from Virginia, encounters a youngster who says, "I couldn't help it; I *had* to do it!" he hands the kid a fist-sized rock from his bookcase.

"Well, let's say that whatever it is that makes you do these things is now telling you that you *must* throw that rock through my window," Doug says, pointing to the window.

75

Confronted with this intervention, youngsters pause a bit, then put the rock back on the bookshelf. Point: We always have more control than we *think* we do.

It's a simple intervention that can be *very* effective. Just be aware that, if you are working with difficult and defiant youngsters, there's a good chance that you'll eventually be picking up glass.

52

"It's Just a Smile; So What?

(But what does it mean?)

A smile should mean that everything is fine and there are no major problems or concerns. But sometimes it can mean, "Don't Go There!"

Since the face is pretty much the show window to the world, folks put a lot of stock in how people *look*, as well as the signals that are passed person-to-person with a look (or the lack of one, as in a downcast face). Counselors make their living reading subtle facial cues and their connection to emotional states both good and bad.

So when a youngster is miserable but smiling, it's a problem. It presents an image to others that is incongruent and confusing. Counselors, because of their training, are in a better position to see the pain under the grin, but a miserable and bright youngster can cover it for a long time. (In the case of adolescent suicide, for example, how many times do we hear folks say, "I had no idea he was that depressed; he was such a happy-looking person.")

I mention all this to infer that, within a school environment, the miserable and grinning youngster might never be referred to you. He certainly *won't* refer himself! If he does come through your door, chances are it will be because of academic or behavioral difficulty, not because he's been depressed for months.

Let me share about Charles. He came to live in a Baptist group home because he could not get along with his new stepmother. All of the circumstances that brought about that placement were extremely disturbing to the boy. (In fact, after his dad and stepmom dropped him off, Charles cried for two hours—something a 13-year-old boy *doesn't* want to do.)

I saw Charles on his third day at the facility. He walked into my office with a wide grin on his face, a good-looking and outgoing kid. I told him it was my intent to meet with all youngsters coming into the home (a true statement) but that, unfortunately, it would have to be a short visit because I had a plane to catch. Then I confronted him:

> *Charles, I love your smile. You should be the poster person for the American Dental Association. But I know for a fact that, when your dad and stepmom brought you here three days ago, you were VERY unhappy. So I'm wondering about the smile.*

> *Charles, I'm going to ask you a question, and I'll make you this promise about the question: You can answer it "Yes" or "No," and when you do answer, I'll ask you no more questions about it today. Understand?*

> *Okay; here's the question. Charles, do you sometimes smile because you really aren't sure what else to do, OR do you sometimes smile because you're afraid that, if you DIDN'T smile, folks would say, "Charles, what's wrong?" and you're not ready to talk about that stuff just yet?*

77

"Yes," he replied.

I thanked him for answering my question, talked a bit about how school was going, then sent him on his way. Everything I did was to set up the *second* visit.

On the second visit, I reminded Charles of his answer to my question. Then I asked him which part of the question fit him the most, the part about smiling not knowing what else to do, or smiling so that folks wouldn't say, "Charles, what's wrong?" and press him to talk about it. (Now we have a question he *can't* answer with a "Yes" or "No.")

"Well, I guess it's a little bit of *both*," he said after a moment of reflection. (The smile was gone; he was now congruent.)

"I'm not sure I understand what you mean, but I want to. Charles, can you help me understand?"

There was a long pause. "I guess it's about my stepmom—actually about *me* and my stepmom."

And we were into it. By the way, did you notice I used four other interventions that are in this book? They were:

1. A brief first visit.

2. A limit of one question

3. An either/or menu (*Splitting the University*)

4. An expressed desire to want to understand and learn about Charles

I've used this basic strategy to get into tough issues with many youngsters. Give it a try; you'll like it.

53

"You Want Me to Do WHAT?"

(Hey, just THINK about it.)

Counseling is really about changing lives by changing the way folks think—about themselves, about others and about the demands of life itself. As thought goes, so goes behavior.

Call it what you want, *Re-thinking*, *Thought Replacement* (Dr. Doug Riley) or *Cognitive Restructuring* (Dr. William Glasser), what we're talking about is a powerful intervention that's not easy to implement.

The reason why change in thought is not easy to implement is that thought, especially in difficult and defiant youngsters, tends to be rigid. Since rigidity of thought is influenced by one's experiences, the replacement or restructuring of that thought has to overcome the impact of a person's psychological and emotional history. That's a tough call.

Here are some statements that are "disguised" in questions. They represent content with which difficult and defiant youngsters often struggle. As you use them as discussion points in your work with youngsters, they will help you get a better picture of where a student's head might be and how you can best work with that youngster.

> *Is being treated fairly important? Do you believe it is a two-way street? Explain.*

> *Just because someone is nice, does that mean they are weak? Explain.*

Is it possible to get revenge over something, but lose too much in the process? If so, what does that tell us?

If I said "I don't know" to EVERY question asked of me, what would others begin to think?

What happens to people who seem never to learn from their mistakes?

I can say, "No one can make me do anything I don't want to do," but does saying that make it really true?

An authority figure prefers to be reasonable, decent and logical, yet his authority is ignored by a few. Why would he have to take stronger measures with people who seem not to care about his effort to be reasonable, decent and logical?

There is a lot of grist for the mill here. Let's look my favorite, the last one. Even difficult and defiant youngsters clearly understand "reasonable, decent and logical," as evidenced by the fact they do substantially better with teachers and administrators who exercise those qualities within their authority. If the youngster *must* do something, like leave the building during a fire drill, and he is asked to do so in an appropriate and reasonable manner, then there is really only one reason why he would still be defiant in his response: He simple wants to *struggle* with authority.

He wants to struggle; there really aren't any other valid reasons. He can't say the principal is being mean, because he isn't. He could say that fire drills are dumb and that the school already has too many of them, but that's pretty grandiose and not really the issue anyway.

So if the issue comes down to the desire to struggle with authority, my question to the youngster would be, "Why would he *want* to struggle with authority? That makes no sense to me. Can you explain it to me?"

My strong guess is that a difficult and defiant youngster would have trouble answering the question, partly because defiance in the face of reasonableness is hard to defend, and partly because their defiance usually runs a lot deeper than a teacher or the school principal. (Even if they have an answer, they'll struggle putting words to it because now you're getting into really uncomfortable stuff.)

You should be able to use this *Re-thinking* approach as an intervention with a youngster one-on-one, but a better benefit would be to use it in a group setting. The group environment affords more opportunity for discussion. (Sometimes there's more discussion than you want!)

54

"Oh, I FORGOT"

(Forgetting IS the problem.)

If you talk with counselors who work with difficult and defiant youngsters, you'll hear them mention how noncompliance is a common problem with these young people. They seem to be strongly compliant-resistant. Checklists, rewards and "systems" really don't work very well over time.

If you talk to them about compliance, that's all it is—talk. These kids are great at talk; they could do it *all day long*. Some are so personable and so talkative they make you wonder *why* you're seeing them in the first place—

until the next report card comes out, or until you see their room at home, or until you catch a glimpse of the pile of trash growing in place on the side of the house. The issue is compliance; the excuse is "I forgot."

Their forgetting is selective, of course. She "forgot" to clean her room, but a promise Mom made her three months ago is retained with crystal clarity.

As a counselor, you will need your own personal compliance issue with the youngster if you intend to open the notion of compliance as a problem. Otherwise, you're dealing with third-party stuff, and your success will be nonexistent or seriously limited. This is where a lot of counselors have trouble.

Make a compliance request from your relationship with the youngster. If he likes to collect baseball cards, tell him you'd like to see one of them:

> *You know, Nolan Ryan has always been a sort of baseball legend to me. He had a great career that spanned from the 60s to the 90s. That in itself is pretty awesome. But I've never personally seen a Nolan Ryan baseball card from when he was with the California Angels. You say you have that one? I'd love to see it. It is possible you could bring it to school tomorrow and show it to me?*

Almost always the youngster will agree to bring the card to school and show it to you, but that doesn't mean it will ever actually make it to school. But if the youngster *does* bring the card to school the next day, consider what that means:

1. He connected with your request, which implies his investment into the relationship.

2. He acted on your request completely on his own. You were not there to remind him to get the card, put it in his backpack and show it to you the next day. He accomplished all of it without prompts (a very important notion).

3. It might not be math homework, but it *is* compliance.

Reinforce the compliance and expand it, if you can. Start out with a day-to-day request, then expand it over several days or even a week. Keep in mind that the longer the time between the request and the time specified for the youngster to honor it (i.e. bring the baseball card), the more time there is for *any* youngster to forget the request. Keep it really simple at first. The issue is to make it a test of compliance, *not* a test of memory.

What does it mean if the student promises to bring something, then only remembers what he'd promised after seeing you the next day? It means he only committed to the request verbally (just like he does with teachers). There was no follow-through, which *is* the problem, isn't it.

At this point the youngster might voluntarily promise to bring the baseball card the next day. See what happens. If the card shows up, good. If it doesn't, then the child is doing the same thing to you he is doing to his parents and teachers: promising a lot and delivering little. Continue to "test" the youngster with compliance requests as you work with him.

Try expanding compliance requests into specifics like, "Will you meet me in the library at the librarian's desk at 3:40 this afternoon." The youngster might tell you she can't do it, and that's fine. But if she says she will, hold her to the agreement.

A little success story. I shared this strategy with a special education teacher who had an unusual challenge. She taught a class for emotionally/behaviorally disordered students, only it was a start-up class. She had only *one* student.

This teacher shared she wasn't sure if she was reaching this student or not. I told her about this little compliance "test," and encouraged her to try it using something that was of interest to the boy. Then I was out of the office for several days.

When I returned to my office, there was a photocopy of a picture of a gosh-awful looking fish on my desk, along with a note from the teacher that simply read, "HE DID IT! See me!"

She told me she learned the boy loved to fish and enjoyed reading about fishing. In their discussion one day, he told her about an article he had read in a fishing magazine about this fish named "Big Daddy." Folks had been trying to land him for years. They would catch him, then he'd break their line and get away. Well, someone finally caught "Big Daddy." He was ugly and *huge*. She asked if he'd bring the magazine so she could see the picture—and he did! Mission accomplished.

55

"I Just Got Back From the MOON!"

(Really? Get any good pictures?)

Before you laugh too much at this one, you must know it actually happened in a counseling session. I asked an 11-year-old boy how his weekend went, and he launched into quite a tale.

He told me that his folks are divorced and that his father lived outside Houston. When he went to visit his dad, they took a trip to the Manned Spacecraft Center. They had a rocket there all fueled up and ready to go, and asked him if he was up for a two-day trip to the moon. He said, "Sure!" and the boy blasted off.

There's a *lot* I don't know about NASA and spacecraft, but I do believe the Houston folks only *track* flights; they don't launch 'em. But I sensed that confronting him would not be productive. Besides, he already knew he didn't *really* go to the moon.

Why would a youngster say such a thing (assuming he wasn't thought disordered or schizophrenic)? I believe it was a cover for his own sense of insignificance. Perhaps he was really saying, "If you really knew how dull and lackluster my life *really* is, you wouldn't waste your breath on me. But if I can tell you some really far-out stuff, just perhaps I can hold your attention a little longer."

I believe there are kids who are starving for just five minutes with us. A little affirmation can work wonders, and it will slowly bring reality back into view and into discussion. It's not a race. Take your time with a youngster like this one.

56

"Why Are You So MAD? I'm Not!"

(It's the DRIP, DRIP, DRIP!)

A lot of difficult and defiant youngsters might not express much anger, but they're carriers! They're quite good at getting *us* to express it.

One of my mentors, Dr. Nick Long, describes this behavior well. He refers to oppositional and defiant behavior by an earlier, sometimes more descriptive title: passive-aggressive. Whenever youngsters work us into full lather and find delight in it, they are doing their best number. Unfortunately, they generally achieve their objectives.

Their's is the Chinese Water Torture of behavior: drip, drip, drip.

These kids pride themselves on making us furious while *they* remain in control. Yet, at the same time, they have difficulty understanding why folks are so angry at them.

I would encourage you to take three approaches in working with youngsters who are passive-aggressive:

1. Show them how their behavior provokes others.

2. Show them how they are very *predictable* in their behavior.

3. Take them out of their comfort zone.

A behavior that creates a response in another person is, by definition, provocative. Even subtle behaviors can be provocative.

Getting into one's personal space is a great example. The next time you have lunch with a friend, and you're visiting after the meal, try pushing your plate past the midline of the table. Watch what she does. We *all* have physical boundaries and want others to respect them.

Remember the girl I mentioned earlier, the one who barricaded herself with pillows on the couch? She was setting boundaries. Had I reached over and took away a pillow, she would have gotten upset. With the defiant youngster, find a way to get into her space enough to make her physically respond. That's provocation. Then talk about it with her, explaining how people can be reactive to even small behaviors of provocation. From there you can move on to some of the youngster's specific passive-aggressive behaviors that upset others.

Be mindful, however, that awareness of one's provocative behavior is not always sufficient to change the behavior. But it is a place to start. Outline some benefits of change the youngster would find appealing.

The very *last* thing difficult and defiant kids want to be is predictable. If you suggest their behavior is predictable, they will likely argue with you. If I can prove to a defiant child her behavior is predictable, what's she going to do? She's going to be *unpredictable* deliberately, just to mess me up. But in doing so, she has to change her behavior into at least one episode of compliance (or something close to it).

I call this approach *Spit in the Soup*. (Is that descriptive enough?) Let's say the girl is always late coming to her session with you. Suggest to her that her tardiness to counseling makes her very predictable. She'll probably deny it, or simply offer excuses for her tardiness. Then suggest to her that you are absolutely *certain* she will be late for the next session. In fact, take out a dollar bill (maybe even one of the origami dollars) and seal it in an envelope in front of the girl. Let her write her name on the envelope, then put it away. Suggest to her that, if she is *not* predicable (shows up on time) at the next visit, she wins the envelope.

This strategy might cost you a buck, but it proves to you and to the student that she *can* show up on time whenever she wishes. It's easy to move this into other examples of predictability, such as not doing or finishing homework. (I'm not suggesting you pay the child for completing homework; you can find other payoffs. It demonstrates to the child that her excuses are usually just excuses, not something she can't control.

It's pretty easy to take the child out of her comfort zone (we've covered a number of strategies that essentially accomplish this). We could take her to a different place for a session, we could bring in another student to make a group of two, lots of things. In the classroom environment, a teacher could put the student on a group project with one or two other students. If she's defiant or noncompliant toward her peers, the teacher should let *them* deal with it. (I've always felt that youngsters have to crank their defiance up a notch to aggravate peers. It doesn't mean they won't do it, but they are less likely to try it with folks their own age.)

57

"Oh, I'm SORRY; I Must Have Dozed Off"

(You did, but you're NOT sorry.)

What about the student who is so aggressive he goes to SLEEP? Now, I've never been in a one-on-one session with a youngster who went completely to sleep, but I've worked with plenty who yawned repeatedly, looked like they could hardly fog a mirror, and complained about how sleepy or tired they were.

I have had a youngster or two go to sleep in a group session. In this situation I generally ask the question, "Is anyone doing something right now that bothers you?" The group will generally take care of it themselves.

My most interesting moment with a youngster going to sleep occurred when I had a conference with his mother. We called the boy in near the end of our conference to discuss his poor achievement in high school. He sat next to his mother, put his head on her shoulder, and fell *asleep*!

She lost it:

> *This is EXACTLY what I'm talking about. Do you see this, Dr. Sutton? He's failing in school and what does he do about it? He goes to SLEEP! I am sick and tired of coming up to the school trying to figure out how we can get him into the eleventh grade when all he does is go to sleep!*

Here was a classic case of passive-aggressive behavior. How on earth can anyone get so upset at a child who is so tired and worn out he just can't stay awake? It's a perfect defense, although the boy delighted in aggravating his mother in this way. He'd never say it, but I'm sure of it.

If you come down too hard on this youngster, he'll haul out his excuses and even make them "fit." If you don't come down hard enough, he'll keep doing it again and again. The solution to the problem is to put responsibility back on him:

> *Yes, I can see that you're not very alert. I'll tell you what. I can work you in for a session tomorrow, but I'll have to check my schedule for an available time. Stop by my office in the morning before school starts and I'll let you know the time and give you an office pass.*

Now you have a compliance issue. You've made the issue of defiance an active process that has nothing to do with fatigue. If the youngster doesn't show up for the time of the session and the office pass, he is being noncompliant. The problem is now on the table instead of on a pillow (so to speak).

58

"Like My SMOKE Screen?"

(Cough!)

In war, smoke is used to confuse the enemy and disguise movement and intent. Some difficult and defiant youngsters are quite good at throwing up a smoke screen in order to send the counselor down another (less painful) path.

They sometimes do this with flattery to get you to talk about something other than a prime issue of theirs. Or it might just be a subtle way to control a session.

Three interventions come to mind regarding smoke screens. One of them is to recognize the smoke screen and give some limited time to it:

I love football, Tom; you know that. I could talk about football and the game this coming Friday until the cows come home. But we need to visit about other issues. So here's what we'll do. I'll set a timer and we can talk football for five minutes. When the timer goes off, the conversation changes. Fair enough?

Another intervention would be to address the smoke screen head on:

I notice that when I ask you anything about _____, you change the subject quickly. Is there a reason for that?

If the youngster truly has difficulty talking about a key issue, you might try a strategy covered earlier: *The One Question Limit*. It would work something like this:

> *I guess I'm a little confused about something that's happening here. I'd like to ask you a question, one question. You can answer it "Yes" or "No" and I promise that, however you answer it, I'll ask you no more questions about it today. Would that be okay? Okay. Here's the question: "Does it make you uncomfortable whenever we talk about _____?"*

This approach allows you to address the issue specifically during the next session. If the youngster indicates that he is uncomfortable whenever the discussion is on a certain topic, then there's no denial to deal with on the next session. On the other hand, if the youngster says the topic *doesn't* make him uncomfortable, then he shouldn't avoid talking about it, right?

59

"Stop the BUTs?

(Please, you've used your quota.)

Counselors learn to go light on giving advice to difficult and defiant youngsters. One, if the advise doesn't work, it becomes the *counselor's* fault. Second, these kids seem to be the world's experts at *The "But ..." Game*. If we suggest that, if a student can't seem to get her homework done when she gets home, she could wake up an hour early and do it in the morning, she has a "But ..." ready:

*Yeah, I see where that would work for most people, BUT I
can't see or read, or write, or talk, or do anything when I
first wake up in the morning!*

And she'll do this with *anything* you suggest. I could go on and on with examples, BUT you get the idea, right?

The *"But ..." Game* isn't unique to young people; adults started it. The advise doesn't ever matter, because it won't work anyway. You eventually get to the point where you don't want to say anything knowing the student will trash it.

A youngster with this negative perspective is very close being in a situation I call *Terminal Uniqueness*. This is a circumstance whereby the young person feels that *nothing* can work for her. It doesn't matter how many other people found solutions or relief for the same concern or problem, those strategies or interventions won't work for her. She's cut herself off from help. Does this sound like a youngster not far from taking her own life? It can become serious stuff. This youngster needs to realize that her needs and problems are *not* that unique.

If you have one of these youngsters on your caseload, you'd probably have more success with her in a group setting. The experiences and the confrontation of peers might help break through her defenses against solutions.

Of course, you could count the number of times she has dismissed your input and challenge her on it:

*Joanie, I have offered three suggestions for bringing up
your grades to passing, and you have dismissed them all.
I'm going to offer one more. Think about it a moment
before you answer.*

If she dismisses the fourth one, consider making one last suggestion:

*Since you've dismissed them all, Joanie, here's what I want
you to do. Reflect on all four of them again and tell me
which of them has the BEST chance of working for you.*

Here you're just trying to derail the *"But..." Express*, but it might work.

If the youngster can handle a bit of sarcasm wrapped around a little humor, you might try this approach:

Joanie, could I please stick your finger with this pin?

WHAT? Why would you want to do that?

*I want to see if your blood is red. You're telling me that
what works for other students won't work for you, so I'm
thinking maybe even the color of your blood is different
from everyone else. What do you think? Green? Purple?
Maybe orange?*

At this point, it's worth a shot—or a stick. But be ready to duck.

60

"Why Am I So MISERABLE?"

(It's because you're getting better.)

It's common for youngsters with issues to worsen a bit before they get better. It can frighten them and cause a counselor to question her approach with that child.

We don't know what we don't know. If a youngster were to repress a lot of emotionally-charged issues, the process of becoming aware of even one or two of those issues could escalate depression and anxiety. Although this is normal, it *doesn't* seem normal to the child. To them it just seems painful.

(The best way I've found to assess repression is to ask the child for their earliest possible memory. Most youngsters can recall back to ages three to six with no difficulty, and those memories are usually pleasant. If an adolescent tells me she CAN'T remember anything earlier than age 10, red flags start popping up. There may be a very good reason why she can't remember anything earlier than that.)

You best opportunity to see a repression breakthrough (which can bring on a sense of loss and sadness) likely will occur in a group counseling setting. And it often happens to the one who's *not* doing the talking.

I remember working with Laura, a 15-year-old who told me she couldn't remember anything earlier than age 11. (This is always a red flag, although it's not that unusual when working with youngsters who are hospitalized or are in long-term residential treatment.) As we were having group, one of the girls was talking about some of her experiences as a small child. I noticed Laura became very quiet and still, and her face became ashen. She had just connected with a memory. What caused it to happen, when she would not have accomplished a repression breakthrough in an individual session? I believe there were three reasons:

1. She felt physically and emotionally safe at that moment.

2. She was attending, without distraction or interruption, to what was being said by a peer.

3. She was able to reflect on her own experiences without any need or pressure to explain them.

Laura was truly shocked that a memory of being six or seven years old came clear to her. Spontaneously, she began to share about her experiences of being raised in a very dysfunctional and abusive family. In later group sessions, Laura got in touch with the sadness of never having her own childhood. She instead lived the unhappy childhood that was *made* for her. She experienced loss, deep loss, but she experienced it appropriately and with support.

As you might expect, Laura was *not* happy about going through these experiences, but she became more and more stable and authentic as she opened, expressed and put closure on a painful part of her life. She got much better and went into foster care within a couple of months.

Laura needed to know that the pain of healing was normal and necessary. I reinforced this in every group session, and the group helped Laura through the pain. But there are a lot of adults who can't or won't do what Laura did. As soon as they get in touch with something uncomfortable, they want to alter the feeling with sex, drugs, work, alcohol—something.

John Bradshaw was the first person I heard who used the term *Salvific Mechanism* to describe the protective nature of repressed memories, especially traumatic ones. (The word "salvific" comes from the same root from where we get words like "salve" and "salvation.") The *Salvific Mechanism* protects us and keeps up functioning whenever we become psychologically and emotionally "overloaded."

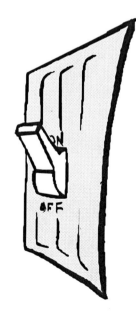

The *Salvific Mechanism* is like a circuit breaker switch that shuts down those painful life experiences we are incapable of handling at the time. In war, for instance, it permits a soldier to keep functioning when he has just seen several of his buddies get killed. "Later!" the *Salvific Mechanism* says to us during these times. "You can't deal with this right now." Unfortunately, many folks don't want to *ever* deal with it, thus all their mechanisms for covering the pain. (See why I like to work with young people?)

Another term young people understand well comes from our experiences with computers—"The Disk is FULL." If our psychological and emotional "storage" is packed to the ceiling, then we can't put any more experiences into it. We have to do a little spring cleaning on the disk first in order to make some space.

You might consider stopping by a hardware store and picking up an inexpensive circuit breaker switch or a light switch. Use it with the youngster to explain why she feels more sad than when she started counseling. Explain to that her that the circuit breaker is now letting the power come through for her to experience feelings more authentically, and that's good. (When you flip the switch or circuit breaker, it makes a "click" to help you punctuate your point.)

You could also use a CD (compact disk) to explain the analogy of "The Disk is FULL." The most valuable supplement to healing for the child, however, always will be your patience, support and assistance.

61 (bonus)

"You CURED Me; Catch You Later!"

(Really? Explain it to me.)

This one happens occassionally with youngsters sent to you, the ones who are not exactly hot prospects for seeing any need for your services.

They might *need* your services, but they don't see it. I've experienced this most often with those youngsters referred to my office through their probation officers. They didn't want any part of counseling.

This youngster knows he has to come for several visits. On the one hand he doesn't want to be there; on the other hand he can't afford to have his probation officer upset with him. (He doesn't care so much about his PO being upset, but he is quite concerned about what his PO might *do* when he gets upset!) So the youngster figures that, if he can convince you that you've accomplished several visits in one with him, he won't have to come back.

"Wow!" the youngster might say. "You are *good*! You are so good you've caused me to see all my mistakes in only *one* visit! You've cured me! I won't need to come back. How could I ever thank you enough?

"Well, for starters," you might reply, "you could tell me what it was I said or did that made such a dramatic difference in only a few minutes?"

Watch him search the ceiling as his mind races for a response. The kid might be excellent in the con game, but he wasn't expecting *this* question.

After a long pause, you get your answer. "It was EVERYTHING!"

With a few decades of experience under my belt, I can assure you it is never *everything* that makes such a difference, if it is genuine. It is something quite specific, a word, an illustration, reassurance—something specific.

If it's genuine, a youngster will always remember what that specific thing was. It was that way with Bonnie. Years after working with her, I saw her in a restaurant. She commented to me how much I had helped her.

"I appreciate that, Bonnie," I said. "But you did the hard work."

"I'll never forget something you told me, Dr. Sutton. I remember it like you said it yesterday. It has helped me more than anything else."

"Goodness, Bonnie, what did I say?"

"You told me that, if I was ever going to get any better, I needed to talk about my problems. I never forgot that."

I thanked her again, but I *didn't* tell her I say that to just about *every* counseling client I've ever had.

The point is that Bonnie, in her gratitude, could be specific. Any person can. If a youngster is profuse with gratitude, yet can't be specific, chances are it's manipulation. Deal with it as such.

I realize that you might not encounter very many youngsters who are this masterful in their manipulative, but you will likely encounter those who will attempt to convince you they no longer need counseling. If they no longer need counseling, it will show up in their lives, their grades and their relationships.

INDEX:

(NOTE: Numbers refer to the number of the intervention, not the page. Pages can be located using the Table of Contents.)

103

Quality Keynotes and Training for Educators

Presented by Dr. James Sutton

■ Most Popular Keynotes

Don't Lose Your Marbles; Give 'Em Away!- This keynote urges participants to become encouragers of young people. The program has a history of successfully delivering a powerful message wrapped in humor and inspiration.

Crossroads to Greatness- Through a compelling story of three pioneers and their guiding principles, this keynote offers insight for planting these principles in the hearts and minds of our young people today.

■ Full-day Training

The Oppositional & Defiant Child- This program will take an intensive look at ways of working with the noncompliant and defiant student, focusing on behaviors of procrastination, pouting and stubbornness, obstructionism and forms of intentional inefficiency, such as "forgetting" and chronic episodes of missing or incomplete school work.

The Kid Who Doesn't Care- This program focuses on working with the socially-challenged student. Behaviors like fighting, lying, stealing and destruction of property will be covered, as well as interventions for more effectively managing this youngster.

Support Staff Training- Dr. Sutton also does full-day training for counselors, social workers and school psychologists on topics relating to depression and anxiety, conducting a diagnostic interview and powerful strategies for group counseling.

■ Half-day Training

The keynote breakout programs listed on the right are half-day (2.5 to 3 hours) training programs also. They have been recently revised and upgraded.

■ About Dr. Sutton

- Nationally recognized psychologist

- Has taught everything from grade school to graduate school

- Committed to platform excellence (*Certified Speaking Professional*)

- Clients include 54 universities

- Bestselling author

■ Add Value; Save Money

Ask about the ***Keynote with Breakout Package***

Breakout programs (about 2 hours) include:

When the Kid Who Can, WON'T- Dr. Sutton addresses the classroom challenges of working with the capable, but difficult, student. There are lots of take-away ideas here.

The Angry Child- Volatile and aggressive youngsters can be a tremendous challenge. This program offers help and hope in reaching the child and improving the behavior!

Addressing Oppositional & Defiant Behavior: Current "Best Practice" Strategies- A program for support staff (counselors, social workers, school psychologists, etc.).

For more information contact:

Dr. James D. Sutton
Pleasanton, Texas
www.docspeak.com

800-659-6628

What others have said:

No way to outclass Dr. Sutton. He holds his audience!
Bob Peterson, San Antonio, Texas

Given the quality of your presentations, I'm not at all surprised that you're in such high demand!
Dean **Charles Wilson**, PhD, Shreveport, Louisiana

Dr. Sutton was an awesome keynoter! He captivated the confer ence participants and most certainly touched every heart. I promise, you could have heard a pin drop during his entire presentation. It was amazing!
Debbie Buchanan, Edinburg, Te:

Additional programs and materials for counselors

"Tell me ..." Skills for Interviewing Children and Adolescents

This program teaches a valuable skill of strategically interviewing children and adolescents. Critical techniques of rapport-building are presented, and the interview protocol is covered in detail as it addresses the ethical practice of collecting information about a child's Life Fields of *School, Peers, Home* and *Community* and *Self.* In all, the interview (*The Life Field Diagnostic Interview*) contains 155 carefully structured questions.

The program, consisting of four audio CDs, workbook and reproducible forms, addresses the interpretation of all parts of the interview. Of special emphasis is the presence of "themes" in the obtained interview, as well as the child's own perspective on issues most needing attention (obviously a great place to start with intervention). Suggestions regarding how this information effectively can be used in the development of goals and plans for service and support (including a child's IEP or Behavior Plan) are also covered.

The *National Board of Certified Counselors* has approved this program for six contact hours of continuing education credit (.6 CEUs) following the successful completion of a quiz over the material. The quiz, as well as all training materials, audio CDs, workbook and *Certificate of Completion* are included in the cost of the program.

What Parents Need to Know About ODD

Although this book was written for parents, it contains the very latest information, insights and interventions on Oppositional Defiant Disorder and similar conditions of defiance and noncompliance in children and adolescents. Counselors and support staff will find this book helpful in their work with difficult, defiant and noncompliant youngsters, and it will be a valuable resource for assisting parents with options and ideas they can use at home.

This book, a major revision and text form of what was formerly an audio program, contains a new section on teaching the oppositional, defiant and noncompliant youngster within the classroom setting. The book is also available in downloadable e-book format at www.DocSpeak.com.

Windows II: A book for those with a heart for helping kids heal

Children often put into behavior what they cannot put into words. Helping them to understand events and circumstances that cause them to experience confusion and fear can be a challenge indeed. And helping youngsters put their thoughts and lives back on track can be tougher still. This book can help.

Through focused questions and activities, the therapeutic stories in *Windows II* provide a counselor ways to 1) assist a child who has been traumatized by hurt and loss, 2) encourage a small group of youngsters to share their experiences in a helping way, and 3) enhance character, understanding and the expression of empathy and support in the classroom.

This book contains a topical reference to the 24 stories in the back, making it handy resource for quick use in individual, group or classroom work. This book is a must for every counselor's reference shelf.

Send, phone or fax order to:

Friendly Oaks Publications
PO Box 662, Pleasanton, TX 78064
(830) 569-3586 fax: (830) 281-2617

Order Form

(Quantity)	(Description)	(Amount)
____	*Interviewing Children & Adolescents ($78.00)*	_____
____	*What Parents Need to Know About ODD ($21.95)*	_____
____	*Windows II ($21.50)*	_____
	8.25% Sales Tax (Texas only)	_____
	Shipping & Handling	__$4.50__
	TOTAL:	_____

Date:_____

Ship this order to:

Name:_____

Address:_____

City:_____

State/Zip:_____

Daytime Phone:_____

Order paid by (circle one): Check   Charge Card

____Visa   ____MasterCard

Card#:_____

Expiration date:_____

108

Printed in the United States
202504BV00002B/1-104/A